Social Media Security for Mobile Devices

How to Protect Your Accounts, Messages, Photos, and Identity on Social Media Apps

By Joe Correa

Published by Live Stronger Faster

This book is for educational and informational purposes only. The author and publisher are not engaged in rendering legal, financial, or other professional advice. Readers should consult a qualified professional before making any financial decisions.

First Edition

Table of Contents

Introduction

Social media has transformed the way people communicate, share information, conduct business, build relationships, and interact with the world. Billions of people now use social networking platforms every day through their smartphones and mobile devices. From sharing family photos and personal milestones to running businesses and networking professionally, social media has become deeply integrated into modern life. Mobile devices have made access to these platforms faster and more convenient than ever before. With a few taps on a screen, users can post updates, upload videos, send private messages, livestream events, and connect with people across the globe instantly.

While social media platforms offer extraordinary opportunities for communication and connection, they also create significant cybersecurity and privacy risks. Every post, photograph, message, location tag, and interaction leaves a digital footprint that can be collected, analyzed, exploited, or manipulated by cybercriminals, scammers, identity thieves, and malicious actors. Many users unknowingly expose sensitive personal information through their social media activity, creating opportunities for criminals to launch targeted attacks, steal identities, gain unauthorized access to accounts, or manipulate victims through social engineering techniques.

Mobile devices have become the primary gateway to social media. Most users access platforms through smartphones rather than desktop computers. As a result, mobile security and social media security are now closely connected. If a smartphone becomes compromised, attackers may gain access not only to the device itself but also to multiple social media accounts, private messages, photographs, contact lists, authentication codes, and personal information stored within applications.

One of the greatest challenges facing social media users today is the misconception that social media security simply means creating a strong password. While passwords remain important, modern cyber threats have evolved significantly. Attackers now use sophisticated techniques including phishing campaigns, account takeover attacks, malware distribution, fake profiles, impersonation scams, credential stuffing, malicious links, deepfake technology, and social engineering manipulation to compromise users. In many cases, attackers never need to hack a device directly because users voluntarily provide enough information through their social media activity to make themselves vulnerable.

Social media platforms are designed to encourage sharing. Users are often rewarded with likes, comments, followers, and engagement when they reveal more about themselves.

Unfortunately, oversharing can provide criminals with valuable intelligence. Details such as birthdays, addresses, family relationships, schools attended, employers, travel plans, hobbies, and financial activities can be pieced together to build detailed personal profiles. This information can then be used to answer security questions, impersonate individuals, launch phishing attacks, or commit identity theft.

The rise of mobile photography has introduced additional risks. Every image captured and uploaded from a smartphone may contain hidden metadata, including geographic coordinates, device information, timestamps, and other identifying details. Criminals can use this information to determine where someone lives, works, travels, or spends time. Even seemingly harmless photographs can reveal sensitive information such as home addresses, vehicle license plates, financial documents, workplace identification badges, or personal belongings visible in the background.

Private messaging applications integrated into social media platforms have also become major targets for cybercriminals. Many users assume that direct messages are inherently secure and private. However, compromised accounts, phishing links, malware attachments, and impersonation schemes frequently spread through private conversations. Attackers often exploit trust between friends, family members, coworkers, and followers to convince victims to click malicious links, download infected files, or provide sensitive information.

Businesses, entrepreneurs, influencers, and content creators face unique social media security challenges. A compromised social media account can lead to significant financial losses, reputational damage, customer distrust, and disruption of business operations. Many organizations rely heavily on social media platforms for marketing, customer engagement, advertising, and sales. Attackers understand the value of these accounts and frequently target them through phishing campaigns, credential theft, and account takeover attempts.

Social engineering remains one of the most dangerous threats in the social media environment. Rather than attacking software vulnerabilities, social engineers target human psychology. They manipulate emotions such as fear, urgency, curiosity, excitement, trust, or sympathy to convince victims to take actions that compromise security. A convincing message from a fake friend, celebrity, company representative, or customer support agent can be enough to trick someone into revealing login credentials or downloading malware onto their mobile device.

The rapid growth of artificial intelligence has introduced both opportunities and risks within social media ecosystems.

AI-powered tools now enable attackers to create highly convincing fake profiles, generate realistic phishing messages, clone voices, fabricate images, and produce deepfake videos. These technologies make deception more difficult to detect and increase the effectiveness of social engineering attacks. At the same time, security professionals are developing AI-driven tools that help identify suspicious activity, detect fraudulent accounts, and protect users from emerging threats.

Privacy concerns have become increasingly important as social media platforms collect vast amounts of personal data. Information regarding user behavior, interests, relationships, purchasing habits, browsing history, locations, and interactions is continuously gathered and analyzed. This data may be used for advertising, personalization, analytics, or other business purposes. Understanding how social media companies collect, store, and share information is a critical component of maintaining digital privacy and security.

Children and teenagers face unique risks on social media platforms. Younger users may be more vulnerable to cyberbullying, online predators, identity theft, scams, misinformation, and dangerous social engineering tactics. Parents and guardians must understand the security features available on mobile devices and social media applications to help create safer online experiences for their families.

Education, communication, monitoring, and privacy controls all play important roles in protecting younger users from digital threats.

Public Wi-Fi networks present another challenge for social media users. Many individuals access social media applications while traveling, working remotely, visiting coffee shops, or using airport networks. Unsecured connections can expose login credentials, browsing activity, and personal data to attackers who monitor network traffic. Combining strong social media security practices with mobile network security measures is essential for maintaining overall digital protection.

Many users underestimate the value of their social media accounts. Even accounts with relatively few followers may contain years of personal information, private messages, photographs, contacts, and behavioral data. Criminals often target ordinary users because they believe these individuals may have weaker security protections than celebrities, corporations, or public figures. Every social media account has value, regardless of the number of followers or level of public visibility.

Digital footprints created through social media activity often persist for years. Posts that seem harmless today may have long-term consequences in the future. Employers, educational institutions, business partners, customers, and even cybercriminals may examine social media histories when evaluating individuals. Understanding how to manage online reputations, protect personal information, and control digital exposure has become a critical life skill in the modern world.

Throughout this book, you will learn how social media threats operate and how to build strong defenses using practical, easy-to-follow strategies. You will discover how attackers exploit social media platforms, how to secure your mobile applications, how to strengthen account protection through authentication tools, how to identify scams and phishing attempts, and how to protect your personal information from unnecessary exposure. You will also learn how to safeguard photographs, messages, contacts, and digital identities while maintaining the benefits of social networking.

The goal of this book is not to encourage fear of technology or social media. Rather, it is to provide knowledge, awareness, and practical skills that allow users to enjoy social media safely and confidently. Cybersecurity is no longer solely the responsibility of technology professionals. Every smartphone user now plays a role in protecting personal information, maintaining privacy, and defending against cyber threats.

By understanding how social media platforms function, how cybercriminals exploit vulnerabilities, and how mobile security practices can reduce risk, you will be better equipped to navigate the digital world safely. Whether you are a casual user, parent, student, entrepreneur, professional, content creator, or business owner, the principles presented in this book will help you strengthen your social media security posture and protect what matters most in an increasingly connected world.

Welcome to *Social Media Security for Mobile Devices*. Your journey toward safer social networking, stronger privacy, and improved digital protection begins now.

Chapter 1

Understanding Social Media Threats and Digital Risks

Social media platforms have become some of the most powerful communication tools ever created. They allow people to stay connected with friends and family, build businesses, promote products, share experiences, and access information instantly. While these benefits are significant, social media platforms also present serious security and privacy challenges. Understanding the threats that exist within social media ecosystems is the first step toward protecting yourself, your family, and your digital identity. Cybersecurity begins with awareness. The more you understand how attackers operate, the easier it becomes to recognize and avoid dangerous situations before they cause harm.

Many people assume that cybercriminals only target celebrities, large corporations, or wealthy individuals. In reality, attackers often prefer targeting ordinary users because they tend to have weaker security practices. A social media account may appear insignificant to its owner, but it can contain valuable information including personal photographs, contact lists, location history, private messages, financial clues, business information, and access to connected applications. Criminals view every account as a potential opportunity for profit, identity theft, fraud, or further attacks against friends and family members.

One of the most common threats on social media is phishing. Phishing occurs when attackers attempt to trick users into revealing sensitive information such as usernames, passwords, banking information, or authentication codes. Social media platforms provide ideal environments for phishing attacks because users naturally trust messages that appear to come from friends, family members, coworkers, or familiar organizations. Attackers often create convincing fake profiles or compromise legitimate accounts to distribute malicious links and fraudulent requests. A simple message claiming that someone tagged you in a photo or shared an important video can lead victims to counterfeit login pages designed to steal credentials.

Social engineering is closely related to phishing but extends beyond technical deception. Social engineering involves manipulating human psychology to gain trust and influence behavior. Attackers exploit emotions such as fear, excitement, curiosity, urgency, sympathy, or greed. For example, a scammer may pretend to be a company representative warning of account suspension unless immediate action is taken. Another may pose as a friend requesting emergency financial assistance. Social engineers understand that emotions often override logical thinking, making victims more likely to comply without carefully evaluating the situation.

Fake profiles represent another major threat across social media platforms. Criminals frequently create fraudulent accounts impersonating celebrities, businesses, government agencies, customer support representatives, romantic interests, or ordinary individuals. These fake identities are often used to build trust before launching scams, spreading malware, gathering personal information, or manipulating victims. Some fake accounts are highly sophisticated and may contain realistic profile photos, detailed biographies, numerous followers, and years of fabricated activity designed to appear legitimate.

Identity theft has become increasingly common in the age of social media. Every piece of information shared online contributes to a person's digital identity. Birthdays, addresses, schools attended, family relationships, employment history, photographs, and travel activities can all be collected and combined by criminals. This information may be used to answer security questions, impersonate victims, open fraudulent accounts, conduct financial fraud, or launch targeted phishing campaigns. Identity theft often occurs gradually as attackers gather small pieces of information over extended periods.

Account takeover attacks are among the most damaging social media threats. In these attacks, criminals gain unauthorized access to a user's account and assume control. Once inside, attackers may change passwords, lock out legitimate owners, send fraudulent messages, steal private information, or use the account to scam followers. Many account takeovers result from password reuse. When users employ the same password across multiple websites, a breach at one service may provide attackers with credentials that work on social media platforms as well.

Credential stuffing is a technique that exploits password reuse on a massive scale. Cybercriminals obtain large databases of leaked usernames and passwords from previous data breaches. Automated software then attempts these credentials across numerous websites and social media platforms. Because many individuals reuse passwords, attackers often achieve success without needing to hack systems directly. This highlights the importance of using unique passwords for every account and implementing multi-factor authentication whenever possible.

Malicious links and malware distribution frequently occur through social media messages, comments, advertisements, and posts. Attackers may disguise harmful content as videos, giveaways, coupons, software updates, news stories, or exclusive offers. When users click these links, they may unknowingly download malware onto their mobile devices. Malware can monitor activity, steal passwords, capture authentication codes, track locations, or grant remote access to attackers. Mobile malware continues to evolve and remains a growing threat as smartphones become central to everyday life.

Privacy invasion is another significant concern. Social media companies collect extensive information regarding user behavior, interests, interactions, locations, and preferences. While some data collection supports platform functionality and advertising, users often underestimate how much information they share voluntarily. Public posts, location tags, profile details, photographs, and interaction histories can reveal sensitive insights about lifestyles, routines, relationships, and personal habits. Understanding privacy settings and controlling information exposure are essential components of digital security.

Location tracking presents unique risks for mobile users. Smartphones continuously generate location data through GPS services, wireless networks, and application permissions. When users share location-enabled posts, check-ins, or photographs, they may inadvertently reveal their current whereabouts. Criminals can use this information to identify daily routines, determine when homes are unoccupied, or track movements over time. Disabling unnecessary location sharing significantly reduces exposure to these risks.

Cyberbullying affects millions of users worldwide, particularly teenagers and young adults. Unlike traditional bullying, cyberbullying can occur continuously and anonymously. Harassment, threats, humiliation, impersonation, and public shaming may have severe emotional and psychological consequences. Understanding platform reporting tools, privacy controls, and account management features helps users protect themselves and others from abusive behavior.

Scams involving investments, cryptocurrency, giveaways, and online shopping have become increasingly common. Social media platforms allow scammers to reach large audiences quickly and inexpensively. Fraudulent advertisements, fake promotions, counterfeit products, and investment schemes often appear convincing because they leverage professional graphics, testimonials, and social proof. Users should approach unsolicited opportunities with skepticism and verify information through trusted sources before taking action.

Artificial intelligence has introduced a new generation of threats. Attackers can now generate realistic images, videos, messages, and voice recordings using AI-powered tools. Deepfake technology allows criminals to create convincing impersonations of public figures, family members, or business executives. These synthetic media attacks may be used to spread misinformation, conduct fraud, manipulate victims, or damage reputations. As AI technology advances, critical thinking and verification become increasingly important skills.

The concept of digital footprints plays a central role in social media security. Every online action contributes to a permanent record of activity. Even deleted content may remain accessible through screenshots, archives, backups, or cached versions. Before posting information online, users should consider potential long-term consequences. Responsible digital behavior helps reduce exposure to future risks and protects personal and professional reputations.

Strong social media security requires a proactive mindset. Security is not a one-time action but an ongoing process involving awareness, vigilance, and continuous learning. Attackers constantly develop new techniques, making cybersecurity education essential for all users. By understanding common threats and recognizing warning signs, individuals can dramatically reduce their risk of becoming victims.

The purpose of this book is to provide practical knowledge that empowers users to navigate social media safely. Understanding threats is the foundation upon which effective defenses are built. In the chapters ahead, you will learn specific strategies for protecting accounts, securing devices, safeguarding personal information, and maintaining privacy while enjoying the benefits of social networking.

Daniel received a direct message on a social media platform

Daniel considered himself reasonably careful online. He used social media daily to stay connected with friends, promote his small fitness coaching business, and share family photos. Like millions of other users, he rarely thought about cybersecurity. His smartphone had become such a natural part of his life that he viewed it as an extension of himself rather than a potential target for criminals.

One evening, Daniel received a direct message on a social media platform from what appeared to be a former college friend. The message contained a simple question: "Is this you in this video?" followed by a link. Curious and slightly concerned, Daniel clicked immediately. The page that appeared looked nearly identical to the social media platform's login screen. Without hesitation, he entered his username and password.

Within minutes, the attackers behind the phishing site gained access to his account. Daniel remained unaware of the compromise until several friends contacted him asking why he was sending strange messages requesting money and promoting cryptocurrency investments. By the time he attempted to log in, his password had already been changed.

The situation worsened quickly. Because Daniel reused the same password across multiple services, attackers were able to access several of his online accounts. His email account became compromised, allowing criminals to reset passwords on additional platforms. Personal photographs, business conversations, customer information, and private messages were suddenly exposed.

As Daniel worked to regain control, he discovered how much personal information he had shared publicly over the years. His profile displayed his birthday, hometown, workplace, family members, and travel history. Numerous photographs contained identifiable landmarks near his home. Public posts revealed details about upcoming vacations and daily routines.

Information he had considered harmless provided criminals with a detailed map of his personal life.

During the recovery process, Daniel met Sophia, a cybersecurity consultant who specialized in helping small businesses and individuals secure their digital lives. Sophia explained that most cyberattacks did not begin with advanced hacking techniques. Instead, attackers typically exploited human behavior. Curiosity, trust, urgency, and convenience often created vulnerabilities more powerful than any software flaw.

Sophia showed Daniel examples of fake profiles that impersonated customer support representatives, celebrities, and business owners. Some accounts appeared remarkably authentic. They contained professional photographs, extensive posting histories, and thousands of followers. Daniel realized that he would have struggled to distinguish many of them from legitimate accounts.

Over the following weeks, Daniel began learning more about social media security. He enabled multi-factor authentication, created unique passwords, reviewed privacy settings, and removed unnecessary personal information from public view. He also started examining every message and link with greater skepticism. Instead of reacting emotionally, he developed the habit of verifying requests before taking action.

As Daniel's understanding grew, he noticed potential threats that previously would have escaped his attention. He identified fraudulent giveaway promotions, fake investment opportunities, suspicious friend requests, and phishing messages disguised as platform notifications. The internet had not become more dangerous overnight. Rather, he had become more aware of risks that had always existed.

One afternoon, Daniel received another message claiming that his account would be suspended unless he confirmed his login credentials immediately. The message contained urgent language designed to create panic. Months earlier, he likely would have complied. This time, however, he examined the sender carefully and recognized several warning signs. The account was fake.

Daniel reported the fraudulent profile and warned several friends who had received similar messages. His experience demonstrated an important lesson: cybersecurity awareness not only protects individuals but also helps protect entire communities. Every informed user makes social media platforms safer for others.

Over time, Daniel began sharing social media safety tips with clients, family members, and friends. Many admitted they had never considered how much information they revealed online. Some discovered weak passwords, public location sharing, or outdated security settings that placed them at risk. Small changes significantly improved their security posture.

Years later, Daniel reflected on the incident that had initially compromised his account. While the experience had been stressful, it ultimately transformed his relationship with technology. Instead of viewing cybersecurity as a technical subject reserved for experts, he understood it as a collection of habits and decisions practiced daily by ordinary people.

The digital world continued evolving. New social media platforms emerged, artificial intelligence advanced, and cybercriminal tactics became more sophisticated. Yet the core principles Sophia taught him remained relevant: think before you click, verify before you trust, protect your personal information, and maintain awareness of potential threats.

Daniel realized that social media security was not about avoiding technology. It was about using technology intelligently. By understanding how threats operate and applying practical defensive measures, users could enjoy the benefits of social media while minimizing risk. The knowledge he gained allowed him to protect not only his accounts and devices but also his identity, reputation, business, and peace of mind.

His journey marked the beginning of a lifelong commitment to digital security. Like many people, he learned that the strongest defense against cyber threats often begins not with software or hardware, but with awareness, education, and informed decision-making. The lessons he learned would continue guiding him through every new platform, device, and technology he encountered in the years ahead.

Chapter 2

Securing Your Social Media Accounts With Strong Authentication and Access Controls

One of the most important steps in protecting social media accounts is securing the authentication process. Authentication is the method by which a platform verifies that a user is truly who they claim to be. Every time you log into a social media account, the platform relies on authentication mechanisms to determine whether access should be granted. Unfortunately, cybercriminals understand that authentication is often the weakest point in a user's security system. Rather than attacking sophisticated computer systems directly, attackers frequently target login credentials because compromising an account through stolen credentials is often faster, easier, and more profitable than attempting to bypass technical defenses.

Many users continue to rely on weak passwords despite years of warnings from cybersecurity professionals. Weak passwords remain one of the leading causes of account compromises worldwide. Passwords such as "123456," "password," birthdays, pet names, sports teams, and family names are easily guessed by attackers using automated software tools.

Cybercriminals maintain massive databases of commonly used passwords and frequently launch automated attacks capable of testing millions of password combinations within short periods of time. A password that seems memorable and convenient to a user may be one of the first combinations tested by an attacker.

Strong passwords serve as the first line of defense against unauthorized access. A secure password should be long, unique, and difficult to predict. Modern security experts recommend passwords that contain at least twelve to sixteen characters and incorporate a combination of words, numbers, and symbols. However, complexity alone is not enough. Password uniqueness is equally important. Using the same password across multiple accounts creates significant risk because a breach involving one service may expose credentials that attackers can reuse elsewhere. This practice, known as password reuse, has contributed to countless account takeovers over the past decade.

Password managers have emerged as valuable tools for improving account security. A password manager securely stores login credentials and generates strong, unique passwords for each account. Instead of remembering dozens or even hundreds of complex passwords, users only need to remember one strong master password. Many password managers also provide security audits that identify weak, reused, or compromised passwords. Mobile password managers integrate seamlessly with smartphones and can automatically fill login forms while maintaining strong security standards.

While strong passwords are essential, they are no longer sufficient on their own. Data breaches, phishing attacks, malware infections, and credential theft campaigns have made passwords increasingly vulnerable. As a result, multi-factor authentication has become one of the most effective security measures available. Multi-factor authentication, often abbreviated as MFA, requires users to provide two or more forms of verification before gaining access to an account. Even if attackers obtain a password, they must still overcome additional authentication barriers.

The most common form of multi-factor authentication involves something you know, such as a password, combined with something you have, such as a smartphone or authentication application. When logging in, users may receive a verification code generated by an authenticator app or sent through another trusted method. This additional layer of security dramatically reduces the likelihood of unauthorized access. Studies consistently show that enabling multi-factor authentication prevents the vast majority of account takeover attempts.

Authentication applications are generally considered more secure than SMS-based verification codes. While text message verification remains better than relying solely on passwords, SMS messages can sometimes be intercepted through attacks such as SIM swapping. In a SIM swapping attack, criminals convince mobile carriers to transfer a victim's phone number to a SIM card under their control. Once successful, attackers can receive authentication codes intended for the victim. Authenticator applications generate codes directly on the device and are not dependent upon cellular networks, making them significantly more resistant to such attacks.

Biometric authentication has become increasingly common on mobile devices. Fingerprint scanners, facial recognition systems, and other biometric technologies offer convenient methods of verifying identity. While biometrics can enhance security, they should be viewed as part of a broader security strategy rather than a complete solution. Biometric systems provide convenience and strong protection against casual attacks, but users should still maintain strong passwords and multi-factor authentication whenever possible.

Another critical aspect of account security involves monitoring active login sessions. Many social media platforms provide tools that allow users to view devices currently logged into their accounts. These features display information such as device types, operating systems, locations, and login times. Regularly reviewing active sessions can help users identify unauthorized access quickly. If an unfamiliar device appears, users should immediately terminate the session, change passwords, and review account security settings.

Account recovery settings deserve special attention because they can become targets for attackers. Recovery email addresses, phone numbers, and backup authentication methods should always remain current and secure. If attackers gain access to recovery channels, they may be able to reset passwords and bypass primary security protections. Users should periodically review recovery settings to ensure they remain accurate and protected.

Social media platforms often offer additional security features that users overlook. Login alerts notify users whenever new devices access accounts. Security notifications may warn of unusual activity, suspicious login attempts, or changes to critical account settings. Enabling these alerts helps users respond quickly to potential threats before attackers establish long-term access.

Third-party application access represents another often-overlooked security risk. Many users connect social media accounts to games, productivity tools, shopping platforms, dating applications, and other online services. Each connection grants permissions that may expose personal information or create additional attack surfaces. Over time, users accumulate numerous connected applications that they no longer use or remember authorizing. Regularly reviewing and removing unnecessary third-party access reduces risk and improves account security.

Attackers frequently exploit trust by creating counterfeit login pages designed to steal credentials. These phishing websites closely resemble legitimate social media platforms and often use convincing branding, graphics, and domain names. Before entering credentials, users should carefully verify website addresses and avoid clicking login links received through unsolicited messages or emails. Accessing social media platforms directly through official applications or manually typed web addresses significantly reduces phishing risks.

Public computers and shared devices present unique authentication challenges. Logging into social media accounts on public systems increases the risk of credential theft through malware, keyloggers, browser caches, or unauthorized access. Whenever possible, users should avoid accessing sensitive accounts from shared devices. If such access is necessary, users should ensure they log out completely and avoid saving passwords or authentication information.

Understanding the relationship between convenience and security is essential. Many users prioritize convenience, enabling automatic logins, saving passwords in insecure locations, or disabling security features perceived as inconvenient. While convenience has value, excessive convenience often creates vulnerabilities. Effective cybersecurity involves finding a balance between usability and protection that aligns with individual risk levels and security needs.

Corporate users, influencers, content creators, and business owners often face elevated risks because their social media accounts may provide access to customers, followers, advertising platforms, and revenue streams. For these users, account security should be treated as a business priority. Compromised accounts can lead to financial losses, reputational damage, disrupted operations, and loss of customer trust. Enhanced security measures are particularly important for accounts with significant public visibility or business functions.

Cybersecurity is not a single action but an ongoing process. Authentication systems, threats, and attack techniques continue evolving. Users should periodically review account security settings, update passwords when necessary, enable new security features, and remain informed about emerging threats. Consistent attention to account security significantly reduces exposure to attacks and helps maintain long-term protection.

By implementing strong passwords, enabling multi-factor authentication, monitoring account activity, securing recovery options, and maintaining awareness of authentication threats, users establish a powerful foundation for social media security. These practices may seem simple, but collectively they represent some of the most effective defenses available against modern cybercriminals.

Rachel paid little attention to cybersecurity

Rachel had spent nearly eight years building her online presence. What began as a hobby sharing healthy recipes and fitness tips eventually grew into a thriving business. Through her smartphone, she managed multiple social media accounts, communicated with sponsors, responded to followers, and promoted online coaching programs. Her social media profiles had become central to both her personal and professional life.

Despite her success, Rachel paid little attention to cybersecurity. She used the same password across several accounts because it was easy to remember. She had heard about multi-factor authentication but viewed it as an unnecessary inconvenience. As far as she knew, nothing bad had ever happened to her online.

One morning, Rachel woke up to dozens of text messages from concerned followers. Several people reported receiving suspicious investment offers from her account. Others asked why she was promoting cryptocurrency giveaways. Confused, Rachel opened her social media application and discovered she could no longer log in.

Panic quickly set in.

After several failed login attempts, she realized someone had changed her password. Her account, which represented years of work and thousands of followers, was now under someone else's control.

Over the next several hours, Rachel contacted platform support and attempted to regain access. During the investigation, she learned that attackers had obtained her password through a previous data breach involving an unrelated website. Because she reused the same password everywhere, the criminals simply tested the credentials on her social media account and gained access.

The attackers wasted no time. They posted fraudulent promotions, sent direct messages to followers, and attempted to scam anyone who trusted Rachel's reputation. Some followers lost money before realizing the account had been compromised.

Feeling overwhelmed, Rachel reached out to her friend Marcus, who worked in information security. Marcus helped her navigate the recovery process and explained how the compromise occurred.

"The attackers didn't hack your account," Marcus said. "They logged in using your actual password."

That realization surprised Rachel. She had always imagined cyberattacks involved highly technical methods. Instead, the criminals succeeded because of a simple security mistake.

After regaining access, Rachel committed to improving her security practices. Marcus guided her through each step. First, she created a strong, unique password generated by a password manager. Then she enabled multi-factor authentication using an authenticator application rather than SMS verification.

The next step involved reviewing active sessions. Rachel discovered login attempts from countries she had never visited. She immediately terminated all sessions and forced every device to reauthenticate. Seeing evidence of unauthorized access made the threat feel very real.

Marcus also helped her review connected applications. Over the years, Rachel had authorized dozens of third-party services, many of which she no longer used. Some had access to profile information, messaging functions, and account management permissions. Together, they removed unnecessary connections and reduced her exposure.

Several weeks later, Rachel received an email claiming her account violated platform policies and would be suspended unless she verified her credentials immediately. The message included a login link that appeared authentic at first glance.

Previously, she likely would have clicked without hesitation.

This time, however, she carefully examined the sender and website address. The domain name contained subtle misspellings designed to mimic the legitimate platform. It was a phishing attempt.

Rachel deleted the message and reported it.

As months passed, she became increasingly comfortable with her new security habits. Multi-factor authentication required a few extra seconds during login, but the inconvenience was minimal compared to the consequences of another compromise. Password management simplified account maintenance, and security alerts provided peace of mind.

One afternoon, Rachel received a notification that someone had attempted to access her account using the correct password but failed the multi-factor authentication check. The attacker likely possessed old credentials from a previous breach. Without the second authentication factor, access was denied automatically.

For the first time, Rachel saw the value of layered security. No single defense was perfect, but together they created formidable protection.

Rachel eventually began sharing cybersecurity tips with her audience. Many followers admitted they reused passwords or had never enabled multi-factor authentication. Inspired by her experience, thousands of people strengthened their own security practices.

The account compromise that once seemed like a disaster became a turning point. Rachel learned that protecting social media accounts was not solely about technology. It involved habits, awareness, and consistent attention to security fundamentals.

Years later, her business continued growing, but so did her commitment to cybersecurity. She understood that every account represented more than a username and password. It represented trust, reputation, relationships, and opportunities built over time.

The lesson remained simple yet powerful: strong authentication is one of the most effective defenses against cybercrime. By taking a proactive approach to account security, users can dramatically reduce risk and protect the digital identities they work so hard to build.

Chapter 3

Protecting Personal Information and Privacy on Social Media

One of the most valuable assets that individuals possess in the digital world is personal information. Every day, millions of people voluntarily share details about their lives through social media platforms without fully understanding the long-term consequences of that exposure. While sharing experiences, photographs, achievements, and opinions can strengthen social connections and build communities, excessive disclosure of personal information can create serious security and privacy risks. Understanding how to manage personal information effectively is one of the most important skills for maintaining social media security.

Social media platforms are designed to encourage engagement and sharing. The more information users provide, the more personalized and interactive the platform becomes. However, every piece of information shared online contributes to a digital profile that may be accessed, analyzed, stored, and potentially exploited. Criminals, advertisers, data brokers, scammers, competitors, and even strangers may gather information from public profiles and use it in ways users never intended. The goal of social media privacy is not to avoid participation but to make informed decisions about what information should remain private and what information can be safely shared.

Personal information comes in many forms. Some examples are obvious, such as full names, addresses, phone numbers, email addresses, and financial details. Other information may appear harmless when viewed individually but become dangerous when combined with additional data. Birthdays, workplace information, schools attended, family relationships, hobbies, travel plans, vehicle information, pet names, and photographs can all contribute to a detailed personal profile. Cybercriminals often collect small pieces of information from multiple sources and assemble them into comprehensive identity profiles that facilitate fraud, impersonation, and targeted attacks.

One of the most common privacy mistakes involves publicly displaying birthdays and birth years. While birthdays seem harmless, they are frequently used as identity verification data by financial institutions, government agencies, healthcare providers, and online services. When combined with other publicly available information, birth dates can help attackers answer security questions or impersonate victims. Limiting public access to birth information significantly reduces this risk.

Family information presents another major privacy concern. Many users enjoy sharing photographs and updates involving spouses, children, parents, and relatives. While these posts may appear innocent, they often reveal names, relationships, schools, activities, locations, and daily routines. Attackers can use this information to build trust during social engineering attacks. For example, a criminal who knows the names of family members may appear more credible when contacting a victim or attempting to impersonate someone within their social circle.

Location information has become one of the most valuable forms of personal data available on social media. Smartphones continuously generate location data through GPS systems, wireless networks, Bluetooth connections, and application services. Many social media platforms encourage users to check in at restaurants, airports, events, businesses, and tourist attractions. While location sharing can be fun and convenient, it also creates opportunities for surveillance, stalking, burglary, and targeted attacks. Sharing real-time location information may reveal where users live, work, exercise, shop, travel, and spend their free time.

Photographs often contain more information than users realize. Modern smartphones automatically embed metadata within images. This metadata may include timestamps, geographic coordinates, device information, and camera settings. In addition, photographs themselves may reveal sensitive details such as home addresses, vehicle license plates, identification badges, financial documents, school uniforms, travel plans, security systems, and valuable possessions. Before posting images online, users should carefully examine both the content of the image and any associated metadata.

Privacy settings serve as critical tools for controlling information exposure. Most social media platforms provide extensive privacy controls that allow users to determine who can view profiles, posts, photographs, stories, friend lists, and personal information. Unfortunately, many users never review these settings and rely on default configurations. Since platform defaults often prioritize visibility and engagement rather than privacy, regularly reviewing and adjusting privacy settings is essential.

Understanding audience selection is a key component of social media privacy management. Users should recognize that not every post needs to be visible to the public. Many platforms allow content to be shared with specific groups, close friends, family members, or approved followers. Limiting audience exposure reduces the likelihood that sensitive information will reach unintended viewers. Developing the habit of evaluating the appropriate audience before posting can significantly improve privacy protection.

Oversharing remains one of the most common causes of privacy-related security incidents. Many individuals post information in real time without considering how it may be interpreted by others. Announcing vacations, sharing boarding passes, displaying new purchases, revealing financial achievements, or documenting daily routines can provide valuable intelligence to criminals. Attackers often monitor social media activity to identify opportunities for theft, fraud, impersonation, or physical crimes.

Social media quizzes and online challenges may appear entertaining but often serve as information collection mechanisms. Questions such as "What was your first pet's name?" or "What street did you grow up on?" frequently resemble common security questions used by financial institutions and online services. Sharing answers publicly may provide attackers with information useful for bypassing account recovery processes. Users should remain cautious when participating in activities that request personal details.

Friend requests and follower approvals require careful consideration. Many users accept connection requests from individuals they do not know simply to increase their network size. However, attackers often create fake profiles specifically designed to gain access to personal information visible only to approved contacts. Reviewing profiles carefully and limiting connections to trusted individuals helps reduce privacy risks.

Data harvesting has become a significant concern in the modern social media environment. Organizations collect information from social media activity to build detailed consumer profiles. These profiles may include interests, purchasing habits, political views, social relationships, browsing behaviors, and lifestyle preferences. While some data collection supports platform functionality and personalized experiences, users should understand how their information is being gathered and utilized.

Mobile application permissions play an important role in privacy protection. Social media applications often request access to contacts, microphones, cameras, location services, calendars, storage systems, and other device features. Some permissions are necessary for functionality, while others may exceed operational requirements. Users should review permissions regularly and disable access that is not essential. Limiting application permissions reduces the amount of data available to platforms and potential attackers.

Children and teenagers require special privacy protections. Younger users often lack the experience necessary to recognize long-term consequences associated with information sharing. Parents and guardians should educate children about privacy risks, monitor online activity appropriately, and establish guidelines regarding what information can be shared publicly. Teaching privacy awareness at an early age helps build lifelong digital safety habits.

Reputation management is closely linked to privacy protection. Information shared today may remain accessible for years or even decades. Employers, educational institutions, clients, business partners, and future acquaintances may review social media histories when evaluating individuals. Before posting content, users should consider how it might be viewed in the future. Responsible sharing helps protect both privacy and reputation.

The concept of digital minimalism offers a useful approach to privacy protection. Digital minimalism encourages users to share intentionally rather than impulsively. Instead of broadcasting every detail of daily life, users focus on sharing meaningful content while maintaining control over sensitive information. This approach reduces exposure while still allowing individuals to participate actively in social media communities.

Privacy is not about secrecy. Rather, it involves maintaining control over personal information and determining how, when, and with whom that information is shared. Effective privacy management allows users to enjoy the benefits of social media while minimizing unnecessary risks. By understanding the value of personal information and implementing thoughtful sharing practices, individuals can protect themselves from many common social media threats.

Ultimately, protecting personal information requires awareness, discipline, and ongoing evaluation. Technology continues to evolve, and privacy challenges will continue changing alongside it. Users who understand privacy principles and apply them consistently will be better prepared to navigate the social media landscape safely and confidently.

Michael loved sharing his life online

As a successful real estate agent, he believed social media was one of the most effective tools for building relationships and attracting clients. Every day he posted updates about his listings, family activities, vacations, fitness routines, and personal achievements. His followers enjoyed the content, and his online presence helped his business grow steadily.

For years, Michael never considered the security implications of what he shared.

One summer, he posted a series of updates documenting a two-week family vacation in Europe. His posts included airport photos, hotel check-ins, restaurant visits, sightseeing adventures, and daily updates from multiple cities. Friends and followers loved the content, and engagement levels were higher than ever.

What Michael did not realize was that someone else was paying close attention.

Several days into the trip, burglars broke into his home.

The criminals had learned through his social media posts that his entire family was out of the country. Public photographs revealed the layout of parts of his home, valuable electronics, artwork, and other possessions. The thieves understood exactly when the house would be empty and took advantage of the opportunity.

The experience shocked Michael.

After returning home and dealing with police reports and insurance claims, he began examining his social media habits more carefully. The burglary was not caused solely by social media, but his online activity had provided criminals with useful information.

Determined to improve his security, Michael attended a cybersecurity workshop hosted by a local technology group. During the presentation, the instructor demonstrated how much information could be gathered from public social media profiles.

The exercise was eye-opening.

Within minutes, participants were able to identify a volunteer's hometown, employer, family members, hobbies, favorite restaurants, travel history, and daily schedule using only publicly available information. The volunteer had never intentionally shared all of that information at once, but years of posts collectively created a remarkably detailed profile.

Michael immediately recognized similarities to his own online presence.

That evening, he reviewed his social media accounts. He discovered that his birthday was publicly visible. His family members were clearly identified. His children's school activities appeared frequently in photographs. His exercise routine followed a predictable schedule that he often shared online. Location tags revealed his favorite coffee shop, gym, office, and neighborhood.

Piece by piece, he realized how much information he had exposed.

Over the next several weeks, Michael began making changes. He adjusted privacy settings, limited audience visibility, removed unnecessary personal details, and stopped posting real-time location updates. Instead of announcing vacations while traveling, he waited until returning home before sharing photos.

His wife, Jennifer, supported the effort and encouraged their children to become more privacy-conscious as well. Together, they discussed the importance of protecting personal information and understanding that not every moment needed to be shared publicly.

Several months later, Michael received a friend request from someone claiming to be a former classmate. At first glance, the profile appeared legitimate. It included photographs, mutual connections, and a detailed biography.

Before accepting the request, Michael examined the account more carefully.

He noticed inconsistencies. Most of the profile photos had been uploaded recently. The account had very little interaction history. The mutual connections appeared to have accepted the request automatically without verification.

Suspicious, Michael contacted an actual former classmate and learned that several people had received identical requests from the same fake profile.

The account was part of a social engineering operation designed to gather personal information from trusted networks.

Because Michael had become more aware of privacy risks, he recognized the warning signs and avoided the trap.

As time passed, he developed a new philosophy regarding social media. Rather than sharing everything immediately, he asked himself a few simple questions before posting.

Does this reveal sensitive information?

Could this expose my location?

Would I be comfortable with strangers seeing this?

Could this information be misused in the future?

These questions helped him make better decisions and significantly reduced unnecessary exposure.

Years later, Michael's social media presence remained active and successful. His business continued growing, and he still enjoyed sharing important moments with friends, family, and clients. The difference was that he now shared intentionally rather than automatically.

He understood that privacy did not require abandoning social media. It simply required awareness and control.

Looking back, Michael realized that personal information was much more valuable than he once believed. Every photograph, location tag, family update, and public comment contributed to a larger digital identity that deserved protection.

The lessons he learned extended beyond cybersecurity. They influenced how he approached technology, communication, and decision-making in general. By protecting his privacy, he gained greater control over his digital life and reduced opportunities for others to exploit his information.

Most importantly, he taught those lessons to his family. His children grew up understanding that privacy was not something old-fashioned or unnecessary. It was a fundamental part of personal safety in an increasingly connected world.

The experience reinforced a powerful truth: information is valuable, and protecting it is one of the most important responsibilities every social media user has. Through awareness, discipline, and thoughtful sharing, individuals can enjoy the benefits of social media without sacrificing their security, privacy, or peace of mind.

Chapter 4

Recognizing and Avoiding Social Media Scams, Phishing Attacks, and Fake Profiles

One of the greatest dangers facing social media users today is the growing sophistication of online scams. Cybercriminals have learned that attacking people directly is often easier than attacking computer systems. Rather than spending time searching for technical vulnerabilities, many criminals focus on manipulating human behavior. Social media platforms provide ideal environments for these attacks because they connect billions of users, encourage trust and interaction, and allow criminals to reach potential victims quickly and inexpensively. Understanding how scams operate is essential for maintaining security on mobile devices and protecting personal information from exploitation.

Scams are designed to achieve specific goals. In some cases, criminals want to steal money directly. In other situations, they seek passwords, financial information, authentication codes, personal details, or access to accounts that can later be exploited. Successful scams often rely on deception rather than technical expertise. The attacker's objective is to convince the victim to take an action voluntarily. This may involve clicking a malicious link, providing sensitive information, downloading harmful software, or sending money under false pretenses.

Phishing remains one of the most common social media threats. Phishing attacks attempt to trick users into revealing sensitive information by pretending to be legitimate organizations, businesses, social media platforms, government agencies, or trusted individuals. A phishing message may claim that an account has been suspended, that unusual activity has been detected, or that urgent action is required to avoid losing access. The goal is to create anxiety and urgency so that victims act before carefully evaluating the message.

Social media phishing attacks frequently arrive through direct messages. A victim may receive a message stating, "Is this you in this video?" or "You won a prize—click here to claim it." These messages often contain links that lead to fake login pages. The counterfeit pages are designed to resemble legitimate websites and may be nearly identical to the real platform. Once users enter their credentials, the information is transmitted directly to the attacker, who can immediately attempt to access the victim's account.

Spear phishing is a more targeted form of phishing. Instead of sending generic messages to thousands of people, attackers customize messages for specific individuals. They may reference a person's employer, hobbies, family members, recent social media posts, or professional activities. Because the messages appear highly personalized, victims are more likely to trust them. Social media platforms provide attackers with valuable information that can be used to create convincing spear-phishing campaigns.

Another dangerous threat is the fake profile scam. Criminals routinely create fraudulent social media accounts that impersonate celebrities, business leaders, customer support agents, military personnel, government officials, or ordinary individuals. These fake profiles are often used to establish trust before initiating scams. Some fake accounts operate for months before attempting fraud. During that time, attackers may post content, gain followers, interact with users, and build credibility.

Romance scams have become one of the most financially damaging forms of social media fraud. In these scams, criminals create fake identities and develop emotional relationships with victims over weeks or months. The attacker may claim to work overseas, serve in the military, or face a temporary crisis that requires financial assistance. Once trust has been established, the scammer requests money, gift cards, cryptocurrency transfers, or other financial support. Victims often continue sending money because they believe they are helping someone they care about.

Investment scams have expanded dramatically with the rise of cryptocurrency and online trading. Social media users frequently encounter advertisements or messages promising extraordinary returns with little risk. Fraudsters may claim that a small investment can be doubled or tripled within days. They often use fake testimonials, manipulated screenshots, fabricated success stories, and counterfeit endorsements from celebrities. Legitimate investments involve risk, and any opportunity promising guaranteed returns should be approached with extreme skepticism.

Giveaway scams are another common social media threat. Criminals may impersonate companies, influencers, or celebrities and announce fake contests. Victims are instructed to click links, complete forms, provide personal information, or send small payments to claim prizes. In reality, no prize exists. The scam is designed to collect information, steal money, or infect devices with malware. Legitimate contests typically do not require winners to pay fees in advance to receive rewards.

Customer support scams exploit users seeking assistance with social media platforms, financial services, online stores, or technology products. Criminals create fake support accounts and monitor public complaints. When users post about problems, the fake support account contacts them offering assistance. The scammer may request login credentials, authentication codes, payment information, or remote access to devices. Because the interaction appears helpful and professional, victims often comply without realizing they are communicating with criminals.

Impersonation scams target trust relationships. Attackers may compromise legitimate accounts or create convincing copies of real profiles. Once established, they contact friends, family members, coworkers, or followers requesting money, favors, personal information, or emergency assistance. Because the requests appear to come from trusted individuals, recipients may respond without verifying authenticity. Whenever unusual requests involve financial transactions or sensitive information, independent verification should always be performed.

Artificial intelligence has increased the sophistication of modern scams. Criminals can now generate realistic profile photographs, videos, voice recordings, and written messages using AI tools. Deepfake technology enables attackers to impersonate real individuals with alarming accuracy. Users can no longer rely solely on visual appearances when evaluating authenticity. Verification through trusted channels has become more important than ever.

Many scams rely on emotional manipulation. Fear, urgency, excitement, greed, curiosity, sympathy, and loneliness are powerful psychological triggers. Scammers intentionally create situations that provoke emotional reactions because emotional decision-making often bypasses critical thinking. Messages demanding immediate action should always be treated with caution. Legitimate organizations rarely require instant responses without providing opportunities for verification.

Mobile devices present unique risks because users often respond quickly to notifications and messages. Smartphone screens display limited information, making it more difficult to examine links, email addresses, or profile details. Attackers understand this and frequently design scams specifically for mobile users. Taking a few extra moments to verify information before responding can prevent many successful attacks.

Recognizing warning signs is one of the most effective defenses against scams. Common red flags include urgent requests, grammatical errors, unrealistic promises, requests for payment through gift cards or cryptocurrency, suspicious links, inconsistent profile information, newly created accounts, and attempts to move conversations to private communication channels. While no single indicator guarantees fraud, multiple warning signs should increase suspicion.

Verifying identities is a crucial security habit. If someone claiming to be a friend, company representative, or family member requests sensitive information or financial assistance, contact the individual through a separate communication channel. Calling a known phone number or using previously established contact information helps confirm authenticity. Trust should never be based solely on social media messages.

Reporting scams benefits the entire online community. Most social media platforms provide tools for reporting suspicious profiles, fraudulent messages, and malicious content. Reporting helps platforms identify and remove dangerous accounts before they harm additional victims. Users who encounter scams should document evidence when appropriate and notify affected friends or family members.

Education remains the strongest defense against social media fraud. Attack techniques evolve constantly, but the underlying principles remain consistent. Scammers seek to exploit trust, manipulate emotions, and create opportunities for deception. Users who understand these tactics are far less likely to become victims. Awareness transforms social media from a dangerous environment into one that can be navigated safely and confidently.

The goal is not to become fearful or distrustful of every online interaction. Rather, it is to develop healthy skepticism and verification habits. By recognizing common scam techniques, evaluating information carefully, and maintaining awareness of emerging threats, users can protect themselves, their families, and their digital identities from many of the most common forms of online fraud.

The account looked authentic

Emily had always enjoyed social media. As a small business owner, she used multiple platforms to market her handmade jewelry and connect with customers. Her social media accounts generated sales, referrals, and valuable business relationships. She considered herself reasonably cautious online, but she had never experienced a serious cyber threat.

One afternoon, Emily received a direct message from an account that appeared to belong to a well-known business mentor she followed. The message congratulated her on being selected for an exclusive investment opportunity available only to successful entrepreneurs. The account looked authentic. It contained thousands of followers, professional photographs, and years of content.

Curious, Emily responded.

The individual explained that a group of investors was generating substantial profits through cryptocurrency trading. Participants only needed to invest a small amount to begin. The mentor's profile displayed screenshots of successful trades and testimonials from individuals who claimed to have doubled their money within weeks.

At first, everything seemed legitimate.

Over several days, the conversation continued. The individual answered questions professionally and never pressured Emily aggressively. This gradual approach helped establish trust. Eventually, Emily transferred a small amount of money to participate in the investment program.

Within days, the online dashboard showed impressive profits.

Excited by the apparent success, Emily considered investing more. Before doing so, she mentioned the opportunity to her brother Daniel, who worked in information technology.

Daniel immediately became concerned.

He examined the profile and noticed subtle differences between the fake account and the actual mentor's verified profile. The username contained a small variation that most people would never notice. The testimonials appeared copied from unrelated websites. The investment platform had no legitimate regulatory information.

The entire operation was a sophisticated scam.

Fortunately, Emily had invested only a relatively small amount. Although the money was lost, the experience provided a valuable lesson. She reported the account and warned others within her business network.

Several months later, Emily encountered another threat.

A customer contacted her business page complaining about a payment issue. Shortly afterward, a profile claiming to represent the social media platform's customer support team sent her a message offering assistance. The representative requested her login credentials to verify account ownership.

Remembering her previous experience, Emily became suspicious.

Rather than responding immediately, she visited the platform's official help center through the mobile application. There she learned that legitimate support personnel never request passwords through direct messages.

The support account was fake.

Emily reported the profile and avoided becoming a victim.

As her awareness increased, she began recognizing warning signs more quickly. She noticed fraudulent giveaways promising expensive prizes. She identified fake celebrity endorsements promoting investment schemes. She recognized phishing messages disguised as account security alerts.

One day, a close friend named Sarah called her in distress.

Sarah had received a message from Emily's account requesting emergency financial assistance. The message claimed that Emily was stranded while traveling and needed money immediately.

Fortunately, Sarah contacted Emily directly before sending anything.

Someone had created a fake profile using Emily's photographs and business information.

The impersonation account looked convincing. Many followers accepted it as legitimate because it used publicly available content copied from Emily's real profile.

Together, Emily and Sarah reported the fraudulent account and notified mutual contacts. The experience demonstrated how easily trust relationships could be exploited by criminals.

Determined to help others avoid similar situations, Emily began sharing cybersecurity awareness tips through her business page. She created educational posts explaining common scams, phishing attacks, fake profiles, and verification techniques.

Her audience responded positively.

Many followers admitted they had nearly fallen victim to scams themselves. Some had lost money to fraudulent investments. Others had clicked phishing links or interacted with fake customer support representatives.

Through education, Emily helped create a more informed community.

Over time, she developed a simple rule that guided her online behavior: trust should always be verified.

Whenever she encountered an unusual request, an extraordinary opportunity, or a message that triggered a strong emotional response, she paused and evaluated the situation carefully. This habit prevented numerous potential problems.

Years later, Emily reflected on how much social media scams had evolved. Criminals had become more sophisticated, using artificial intelligence, professional branding, and psychological manipulation to deceive victims. Yet despite these advances, the fundamental defense remained the same.

Awareness.

By understanding how scams operate, recognizing warning signs, and verifying information before taking action, users can avoid many of the most common threats.

Emily continued using social media successfully to grow her business and connect with customers. The difference was that she now approached online interactions with confidence rather than blind trust.

She understood that social media could be both a valuable tool and a dangerous environment. The key was learning how to recognize deception before it caused harm.

The lessons she learned protected not only her finances but also her reputation, relationships, and peace of mind. Through vigilance, education, and thoughtful decision-making, she transformed from a potential victim into a knowledgeable and resilient digital citizen.

Her experience serves as a reminder that cybercriminals may constantly invent new scams, but informed users will always possess the strongest defense: the ability to recognize manipulation and choose security over impulse.

Chapter 5

Protecting Photos, Messages, and Shared Content on Social Media

Every day, billions of photographs, videos, messages, comments, stories, and posts are shared across social media platforms. Mobile devices have made content creation easier than ever before. With a smartphone in hand, users can instantly capture moments, communicate with friends, document experiences, promote businesses, and share information with audiences around the world. While this convenience has transformed communication, it has also created significant security and privacy challenges. Understanding how to protect shared content is essential for maintaining control over personal information and reducing exposure to cyber threats.

Many users assume that content shared with friends or followers remains private. In reality, once information is posted online, control over that content can become extremely limited. Even if privacy settings restrict access to specific audiences, recipients can take screenshots, download media, record content, or redistribute information to others. A message intended for a single person can quickly spread to hundreds or thousands of people. Therefore, one of the most important principles of social media security is understanding that anything shared online has the potential to become public.

Photographs are among the most commonly shared forms of social media content. While images may appear harmless, they often contain significant amounts of sensitive information. Family photographs can reveal names, relationships, locations, schools, workplaces, hobbies, and daily routines. Images taken inside homes may expose security systems, valuable possessions, personal documents, financial information, or identifying details visible in the background. Before posting photographs online, users should carefully review the entire image for information that could be exploited by criminals or used to compromise privacy.

Metadata presents another important consideration when sharing photographs. Modern smartphones automatically attach metadata to images. This data may include timestamps, device details, camera settings, and geographic coordinates. Location metadata can reveal exactly where a photograph was taken, even if the location is not visible within the image itself. Many social media platforms remove some metadata during uploads, but users should not assume that all identifying information is eliminated. Reviewing privacy settings and disabling unnecessary location tagging can help reduce exposure.

Children's photographs require special attention. Parents naturally enjoy sharing milestones, achievements, school events, and family moments. However, excessive sharing of children's information may create long-term privacy concerns. Criminals can collect names, schools, routines, interests, and family details from public posts. In some cases, photographs may be copied and misused without parental knowledge. Before posting images involving children, parents should carefully evaluate audience settings and consider limiting public visibility.

Videos often reveal even more information than photographs. Background conversations, street signs, vehicle license plates, business names, computer screens, financial documents, and home layouts may all be visible within video recordings. Because videos contain multiple frames and audio content, users should review recordings carefully before posting them online. What appears insignificant during recording may reveal valuable information when analyzed later.

Private messaging platforms have become central components of social media ecosystems. Many users treat direct messages as secure environments where conversations remain confidential. While private messaging can provide greater privacy than public posts, messages are not immune to risks. Compromised accounts, device theft, malware infections, screenshots, and unauthorized access can all expose private communications. Users should avoid sharing highly sensitive information through messaging platforms unless absolutely necessary.

One of the most common mistakes involves sending confidential information through direct messages. Financial account numbers, passwords, authentication codes, personal identification documents, medical information, and sensitive business data should rarely be transmitted through social media messaging systems. Even when messages appear private, multiple factors may compromise their security. Whenever possible, sensitive communications should utilize secure and trusted channels specifically designed for confidential information.

Temporary content features such as stories and disappearing messages have created a false sense of security for some users. While these features automatically remove content after a specified period, recipients may still capture screenshots, record screens, or use external devices to preserve information permanently. Users should never assume that temporary content is truly temporary. The safest approach is to share only content that would not cause harm if preserved indefinitely.

Social media platforms encourage engagement through comments, reactions, tags, and mentions. While these features enhance interaction, they can also expose users to privacy risks. Tagging individuals in photographs or posts may reveal locations, relationships, and activities without their consent. Respecting the privacy preferences of friends, family members, coworkers, and business associates helps maintain trust and reduces unnecessary exposure.

Cloud synchronization introduces both benefits and risks. Many social media applications automatically synchronize photographs, videos, and messages across multiple devices and cloud storage systems. While synchronization provides convenience and backup protection, it also expands the number of locations where data is stored. Each additional storage location creates potential security risks. Users should understand how synchronization functions and review associated privacy settings regularly.

Content theft has become increasingly common across social media platforms. Photographs, videos, articles, artwork, and other creative works are frequently copied and redistributed without permission. Business owners, influencers, content creators, and professionals should consider watermarking valuable content and monitoring unauthorized use when appropriate. Although complete prevention may be impossible, awareness helps users take reasonable protective measures.

Cybercriminals often use shared content as a source of intelligence. A single photograph may reveal travel plans, expensive purchases, business activities, family relationships, or financial success. Criminals combine information from multiple posts to build detailed profiles of potential victims. This information can support identity theft, phishing attacks, impersonation scams, and other forms of fraud. Thoughtful content sharing significantly reduces the amount of intelligence available to attackers.

Reputation management is closely linked to content protection. Every post contributes to a digital footprint that may persist for years. Content shared impulsively during moments of anger, excitement, frustration, or emotional stress can have lasting consequences. Employers, clients, educational institutions, business partners, and future acquaintances may review social media histories when evaluating individuals. Developing habits of thoughtful posting helps protect both personal and professional reputations.

Social media platforms provide privacy controls that allow users to manage who can view content. Options may include public visibility, friends-only access, custom audiences, close friend lists, or restricted groups. Regularly reviewing these settings helps ensure that content reaches intended audiences while minimizing unnecessary exposure. Privacy controls are valuable tools, but they should be combined with responsible sharing practices rather than viewed as complete solutions.

Content archiving and deletion deserve careful consideration. Many users believe that deleting a post removes it permanently. In reality, copies may remain on servers, backups, screenshots, archives, search engine caches, or third-party systems. Before publishing content, users should consider whether they would be comfortable with the information remaining accessible indefinitely. Prevention is often more effective than attempting to remove content later.

Education and awareness remain essential components of content security. Technology continues evolving, and new methods of sharing information emerge regularly. Understanding how content can be viewed, copied, analyzed, and exploited empowers users to make informed decisions. Social media should enhance communication and relationships rather than create unnecessary risks.

Ultimately, protecting photos, messages, and shared content involves balancing openness with caution. Social media can provide tremendous value when used responsibly. By evaluating content carefully before sharing, controlling audience visibility, respecting privacy, and understanding potential risks, users can enjoy the benefits of digital communication while maintaining greater control over their information and identities.

Olivia loved capturing moments

Whether she was traveling, spending time with friends, attending business events, or enjoying family gatherings, her smartphone was always nearby. Social media served as her digital scrapbook. Every memorable experience found its way online through photographs, videos, stories, and updates.

As a successful marketing consultant, Olivia had built a large online following. Her content showcased professional accomplishments, lifestyle experiences, and behind-the-scenes glimpses of her daily life. Followers appreciated her authenticity, and her online presence contributed significantly to her business success.

For years, everything seemed harmless.

One afternoon, Olivia posted a photograph celebrating the purchase of a new luxury vehicle. The image received hundreds of positive comments and reactions. Excited by the attention, she shared additional photos documenting the purchase process and included a short video tour of the vehicle.

Several weeks later, she received a call from her insurance company.

Someone had attempted to impersonate her and obtain information regarding the vehicle. Investigators believed the criminals gathered details from publicly available social media content. The photographs contained more information than Olivia realized, including partial documentation visible in the background and identifiable dealership information.

Fortunately, no financial loss occurred, but the incident was unsettling.

Curious about how much information her content revealed, Olivia began reviewing her previous posts. She was surprised by what she discovered.

Vacation photographs revealed travel schedules. Family pictures identified relatives by name. Videos recorded inside her home displayed expensive electronics, artwork, and portions of her security system. Some posts contained location tags that documented her daily routine with remarkable accuracy.

Individually, the posts appeared harmless.

Collectively, they painted a detailed picture of her life.

Determined to learn more, Olivia attended a cybersecurity seminar focused on social media privacy. During one exercise, participants analyzed fictional social media profiles to identify potential security risks.

The results were eye-opening.

Using only publicly available information, participants successfully estimated home locations, work schedules, family structures, hobbies, income levels, and travel habits. The exercise demonstrated how criminals gather intelligence from seemingly ordinary content.

Inspired to improve her security practices, Olivia began making changes.

She adjusted privacy settings and limited audience visibility for personal posts. She stopped sharing real-time travel updates and instead posted vacation photos after returning home. She reviewed old content and removed posts that revealed unnecessary personal details.

One day, her younger cousin Mia contacted her with a concern.

Someone had created a fake profile using Olivia's photographs.

The fraudulent account copied images directly from her public posts and used them to impersonate her. The scammer contacted followers, promoted fake investment opportunities, and attempted to collect money from unsuspecting victims.

Although the account was eventually removed, the experience demonstrated how easily publicly shared content could be misused.

Several months later, Olivia encountered another lesson.

While organizing old photographs, she discovered images containing documents visible in the background. One photograph showed part of a boarding pass. Another included a conference badge displaying contact information. Several contained computer screens showing business data.

None of these details had attracted her attention when the photos were originally posted.

Now she understood their significance.

As her awareness grew, Olivia adopted a simple review process before sharing content. She examined images carefully for sensitive information, considered audience visibility, and evaluated whether the content could create privacy or security risks.

These habits soon became automatic.

One evening, a friend named Sarah prepared to post photographs from a family event. Olivia noticed that one image clearly displayed children's school uniforms, complete with the school's name and logo.

Sarah had not noticed.

Grateful for the observation, she selected different photographs for sharing.

Moments like these reinforced how easily information could be exposed unintentionally.

Over time, Olivia became an advocate for responsible social media sharing. She taught friends, family members, and business clients how to evaluate content from a security perspective. Many were surprised to learn how much information criminals could gather from photographs, videos, and public posts.

The more she learned, the more she appreciated the value of intentional sharing.

She did not stop using social media. She continued documenting important moments, promoting her business, and connecting with others. The difference was that she approached content creation with awareness rather than impulse.

Years later, Olivia reflected on how her relationship with social media had evolved. She realized that security did not require secrecy or isolation. Instead, it involved understanding how information flows through digital environments and making informed decisions about what to share.

Her online presence remained authentic, engaging, and successful. At the same time, it became significantly safer.

The lessons she learned extended far beyond photographs and messages. They taught her that every piece of content carries potential value—not only for intended audiences but also for individuals with harmful intentions.

By exercising caution, reviewing content carefully, and maintaining control over personal information, Olivia protected herself from many risks that others overlooked.

Her experience demonstrated a powerful truth about social media security: once content is shared, control becomes limited. The best protection comes from thoughtful decisions made before posting rather than attempts to undo exposure afterward.

Through awareness, discipline, and responsible sharing, users can enjoy the benefits of social media while safeguarding their privacy, security, and digital identities for years to come.

Chapter 6

Mobile Device Security for Social Media Protection

Social media security begins long before a user opens a social networking application. While many people focus on protecting their accounts, passwords, and privacy settings, they often overlook the device itself. Smartphones and tablets serve as the primary gateways to social media platforms, making them one of the most important components of a user's overall security strategy. If a mobile device becomes compromised, attackers may gain access to social media accounts, private messages, photographs, contacts, authentication applications, financial information, and numerous other forms of sensitive data. Understanding how to secure mobile devices is therefore essential for protecting social media activity.

Modern smartphones function as powerful computers that store vast amounts of personal information. In addition to social media applications, mobile devices often contain email accounts, banking applications, digital wallets, authentication tools, business communications, health information, location histories, and cloud storage access. Because so much information is concentrated in a single device, smartphones have become highly attractive targets for cybercriminals. A compromised device may provide attackers with access to multiple accounts and services simultaneously.

One of the most fundamental security measures is maintaining a strong device lock screen. Many users still rely on simple PIN codes such as 1234, 1111, or birth years. These codes are easy to guess and offer limited protection against unauthorized access. Stronger authentication methods include complex passcodes, biometric authentication, or combinations of both. A secure lock screen serves as the first barrier protecting all information stored on the device.

Biometric authentication has become increasingly common on modern smartphones. Fingerprint recognition and facial recognition systems provide convenient ways to secure devices while maintaining ease of use. Although biometric systems are not perfect, they generally provide stronger protection than weak PINs or simple passwords. When combined with strong passcodes, biometric authentication can significantly improve device security and reduce the likelihood of unauthorized access.

Operating system updates play a critical role in mobile security. Smartphone manufacturers and software developers continuously identify and correct security vulnerabilities.

These vulnerabilities may allow attackers to bypass security controls, install malware, access sensitive information, or gain unauthorized control over devices. Security updates often address these weaknesses before they can be widely exploited. Users who delay updates may remain exposed to known vulnerabilities that have already been patched by developers.

Application updates are equally important. Social media platforms, messaging applications, browsers, and other mobile software frequently receive security improvements. Attackers often target outdated applications because known vulnerabilities may provide opportunities for exploitation. Enabling automatic updates helps ensure that applications remain protected against emerging threats while reducing the burden of manual maintenance.

Malware remains one of the most serious threats facing mobile users. Mobile malware includes malicious software designed to steal information, monitor activity, intercept communications, display fraudulent advertisements, or provide remote access to attackers. Some malware targets social media users specifically by capturing login credentials, monitoring messages, or stealing authentication codes. Mobile malware can spread through malicious applications, compromised websites, phishing links, infected advertisements, or unauthorized downloads.

Application installation practices significantly influence device security. Official application stores typically implement security screening processes designed to identify malicious software before distribution. While these systems are not perfect, they provide substantially greater protection than unofficial sources. Users should avoid downloading applications from unknown websites, unverified marketplaces, or suspicious links shared through social media messages. Restricting installations to trusted sources reduces malware exposure considerably.

Application permissions deserve careful attention. Many applications request access to device features such as cameras, microphones, contacts, location services, storage systems, calendars, and messaging functions. While some permissions are necessary for proper functionality, others may exceed operational requirements. Excessive permissions increase privacy risks and create opportunities for abuse if applications become compromised. Regularly reviewing permissions and disabling unnecessary access helps maintain stronger control over personal information.

Public Wi-Fi networks introduce additional security concerns. Social media users frequently connect to wireless networks in airports, hotels, coffee shops, restaurants, shopping centers, and public spaces. While convenient, public networks may expose users to various attacks. Criminals can create fraudulent wireless networks that mimic legitimate services or intercept communications transmitted over unsecured connections. Users should exercise caution when accessing social media accounts through unfamiliar networks.

Virtual Private Networks, commonly known as VPNs, provide an additional layer of protection when using public networks. VPNs encrypt internet traffic between devices and remote servers, making it more difficult for attackers to monitor activity or intercept sensitive information. Although VPNs do not solve every security problem, they can significantly improve privacy and security when accessing social media platforms through potentially risky networks.

Device encryption is another valuable security feature. Modern smartphones typically support encryption technologies that protect stored information from unauthorized access. Encryption converts data into unreadable formats that require authentication credentials to access. If a device is lost or stolen, encryption helps prevent criminals from extracting sensitive information directly from storage systems.

Physical security remains an often-overlooked component of cybersecurity. No software solution can fully compensate for poor physical security practices. Leaving devices unattended in public places, sharing devices with untrusted individuals, or failing to secure smartphones during travel increases exposure to theft and unauthorized access. Treating mobile devices as valuable assets and maintaining physical control over them is essential for protecting social media accounts and personal information.

Remote management features provide important protection against device loss or theft. Most smartphone operating systems include tools that allow users to locate devices, display messages, lock systems remotely, or erase data if recovery becomes impossible. Enabling these features before problems occur ensures that users can respond quickly during emergencies. The ability to remotely secure a device can significantly reduce the impact of theft or loss.

Backup strategies are equally important. Mobile devices may be damaged, stolen, infected with malware, or affected by technical failures. Regular backups help preserve photographs, contacts, messages, settings, and other valuable information. Cloud-based backup systems and encrypted local backups both offer effective protection against data loss. Maintaining current backups ensures that users can recover information without relying on compromised devices.

Social media applications often remain logged in for convenience. While this feature improves usability, it also increases risk if devices are lost, stolen, or accessed by unauthorized individuals. Users should understand which accounts remain active and consider implementing additional authentication requirements for sensitive applications. Some platforms support biometric verification before opening social media applications, providing another layer of protection.

Security awareness remains the foundation of effective mobile protection. Attackers continually develop new techniques designed to compromise devices and exploit user behavior. No security tool can eliminate all risks. However, informed users who understand common threats, maintain secure devices, install updates promptly, review permissions carefully, and practice responsible online behavior dramatically reduce their exposure to attacks.

Ultimately, mobile device security and social media security are inseparable. Social media accounts depend upon the integrity of the devices used to access them. A secure smartphone provides a strong foundation upon which all other security measures are built. By protecting mobile devices, users strengthen the security of their accounts, communications, personal information, and digital identities.

Developing strong device security habits requires consistency rather than perfection. Small actions performed regularly—such as installing updates, reviewing permissions, enabling encryption, and maintaining backups—collectively provide substantial protection. These habits help transform mobile devices from potential vulnerabilities into powerful tools for secure communication and social networking.

Jason considered himself highly knowledgeable about technology

As a sales manager for a growing company, he relied heavily on his smartphone. The device contained business emails, customer contacts, financial applications, social media accounts, and countless personal photographs. Because he used the phone constantly, he valued convenience above all else.

His lock screen consisted of a simple four-digit PIN.

Automatic application updates were disabled because he disliked interruptions.

Several applications had permissions he never reviewed.

For years, these habits seemed harmless.

One afternoon, while traveling for a business conference, Jason stopped at a busy airport terminal. While waiting for his flight, he connected to a free public Wi-Fi network labeled "Airport Guest WiFi."

The network appeared legitimate.

Unbeknownst to Jason, the wireless network had been created by a cybercriminal operating nearby. The fake network was designed to capture internet traffic from unsuspecting travelers.

During the next hour, Jason checked social media accounts, reviewed email messages, and logged into several online services.

Nothing appeared unusual.

Several days later, however, strange activity began appearing across multiple accounts.

Friends reported receiving unusual social media messages. Password reset notifications arrived unexpectedly. Some online services detected login attempts from unfamiliar locations.

Concerned, Jason contacted his friend Megan, a cybersecurity consultant.

After reviewing the situation, Megan identified several security weaknesses. The compromised wireless network may have captured sensitive information. More importantly, Jason's device lacked many basic security protections that could have limited potential damage.

Megan helped Jason perform a complete security assessment.

The results were eye-opening.

His operating system was several versions behind on security updates.

Multiple applications had unnecessary access to contacts, microphones, and location services.

Important accounts lacked multi-factor authentication.

Several applications had not been updated in months.

Most concerning of all, his device contained a malicious application that had likely been installed through an advertisement months earlier.

The malware monitored activity quietly in the background.

Fortunately, the infection was detected before causing major financial damage.

Together, Jason and Megan began rebuilding his security posture.

First, they removed suspicious applications and installed pending updates. Next, they enabled device encryption, activated biometric authentication, and created a stronger passcode. They reviewed application permissions one by one, removing unnecessary access wherever possible.

Jason also enabled remote device management features and verified that backups were functioning correctly.

The process required several hours, but the improvements were substantial.

Over the following weeks, Jason became increasingly interested in cybersecurity. He learned how attackers exploit outdated software, malicious applications, and insecure networks. He discovered that many cyberattacks succeed not because technology fails but because users underestimate risks.

Several months later, another incident reinforced the importance of his new habits.

While attending a conference in another city, Jason accidentally left his smartphone in a rideshare vehicle.

Immediately realizing the mistake, he used a secondary device to access remote management features. He located the phone, displayed contact information on the lock screen, and secured the device remotely.

Although the phone was eventually returned, the experience demonstrated how valuable those security tools could be during emergencies.

A year later, Jason's company launched a social media marketing initiative involving dozens of employees. Because of his experiences, management asked him to help develop mobile security guidelines.

Jason shared practical lessons learned through personal experience.

Keep devices updated.

Use strong authentication.

Review permissions regularly.

Avoid untrusted applications.

Exercise caution on public networks.

Enable backups and remote security features.

Protect physical access to devices.

The recommendations were simple but effective.

Many employees implemented changes immediately, improving security across the organization.

Looking back, Jason realized that he had once viewed cybersecurity as something relevant only to large corporations and technology experts. The airport incident changed that perspective completely.

He now understood that every smartphone represents a valuable target.

The device contains personal information, financial access, social media accounts, business communications, and digital identities. Protecting that information requires ongoing attention and responsible habits.

Most importantly, Jason learned that security is not about eliminating convenience. It is about making informed choices that balance usability with protection.

His smartphone remained an essential part of daily life. He continued using social media, managing business operations, and staying connected with family and friends. The difference was that he now did so with confidence rather than complacency.

The lessons he learned transformed his approach to technology and helped protect not only his own information but also the people around him.

His experience illustrates a simple but powerful reality: securing social media accounts begins with securing the devices used to access them. When mobile devices are protected properly, they become strong foundations for safe communication, secure networking, and responsible participation in the digital world.

In an age where smartphones serve as gateways to nearly every aspect of life, protecting the device itself may be one of the most important cybersecurity decisions a person can make.

Chapter 7

Building Long-Term Social Media Security Habits and Digital Resilience

Social media security is not a single action, software program, or privacy setting. It is a continuous process that requires awareness, discipline, and adaptation. Many users focus on immediate security measures such as creating strong passwords, enabling multi-factor authentication, adjusting privacy settings, or avoiding phishing scams. While these actions are essential, long-term protection depends upon developing habits that remain effective as technology evolves and new threats emerge. Building digital resilience means creating a mindset and lifestyle that support ongoing security rather than relying on isolated defensive measures.

Digital resilience refers to the ability to anticipate, withstand, recover from, and adapt to cybersecurity challenges. In the context of social media, resilience involves maintaining control over accounts, protecting personal information, recovering from incidents efficiently, and continuing to use technology safely despite changing risks. Just as physical health depends on consistent habits rather than occasional exercise, cybersecurity depends on routine practices performed regularly over time.

One of the most important habits is maintaining cybersecurity awareness. Threats evolve continuously. New scams, phishing techniques, malware variants, social engineering tactics, and privacy challenges appear every year. Users who stop learning eventually become vulnerable because attackers constantly adapt their methods. Staying informed about emerging threats allows individuals to recognize risks before becoming victims. Reading security news, following trusted cybersecurity resources, and reviewing platform security updates periodically can significantly improve awareness.

Regular account reviews should become part of every user's security routine. Many people configure social media settings once and never revisit them. However, platforms frequently introduce new features, modify privacy options, and update security controls. Users should periodically review account settings, privacy preferences, authentication methods, connected applications, and login activity. These reviews help identify potential vulnerabilities before they can be exploited.

Password hygiene remains a critical long-term security habit. Even when strong passwords are initially created, users should continue monitoring account security. Password managers can help identify compromised credentials, reused passwords, and weak authentication practices. While security experts no longer recommend changing passwords unnecessarily, users should update credentials whenever compromise is suspected or confirmed. Maintaining unique passwords across all accounts remains one of the most effective ways to reduce risk.

Multi-factor authentication should become a permanent component of account security rather than a temporary precaution. Some users enable additional authentication only after experiencing a security incident. However, waiting until after a compromise occurs defeats much of its protective value. Long-term security requires proactive measures. Once enabled, multi-factor authentication should remain active and be reviewed periodically to ensure backup methods and recovery options remain current.

Digital minimalism offers another valuable approach to long-term security. Digital minimalism encourages users to reduce unnecessary exposure by sharing information intentionally rather than impulsively. Many security risks originate from excessive disclosure of personal details, locations, activities, relationships, and opinions. By sharing thoughtfully and limiting unnecessary exposure, users reduce the amount of information available to attackers. This approach does not require abandoning social media; rather, it promotes mindful participation.

Emotional awareness plays an important role in cybersecurity. Many successful attacks exploit emotions such as fear, urgency, excitement, anger, curiosity, loneliness, or greed. Attackers understand that emotional reactions often bypass logical thinking. Developing the habit of pausing before responding to unexpected messages, offers, requests, or opportunities can prevent many scams. A brief moment of reflection often provides enough time to recognize warning signs that would otherwise be overlooked.

Managing digital footprints is another essential long-term practice. Every social media post contributes to an individual's online identity. Over time, years of content can reveal personal habits, interests, locations, relationships, financial circumstances, and behavioral patterns. Users should periodically review older content and consider whether it still aligns with their privacy goals, professional image, and personal values. Cleaning up outdated or unnecessary content helps maintain greater control over digital reputations.

Backup and recovery planning are frequently overlooked aspects of resilience. Even the most secure accounts may eventually face challenges such as device failures, forgotten passwords, accidental deletions, account lockouts, or unauthorized access attempts. Maintaining backups of important photographs, videos, contacts, and communications ensures that valuable information remains accessible regardless of unforeseen circumstances. Recovery planning also includes maintaining updated contact information and secure access to recovery methods.

Building secure social networks involves evaluating relationships carefully. Social media platforms often encourage users to maximize connections, followers, and interactions. However, larger networks are not always safer networks. Accepting connection requests from strangers increases exposure to fake profiles, scammers, social engineers, and malicious actors. Long-term security benefits from cultivating trusted digital relationships rather than prioritizing quantity over quality.

Children and family members play important roles in overall digital security. A family's security is often only as strong as its least informed member. Teaching cybersecurity principles to children, teenagers, spouses, and older relatives helps create safer digital environments for everyone. Family discussions regarding privacy, scams, social media behavior, and online safety can significantly reduce collective risk. Education remains one of the most effective forms of protection available.

Balancing convenience and security requires ongoing attention. Technology companies frequently prioritize convenience because users value seamless experiences. Automatic logins, persistent sessions, synchronized devices, and simplified authentication improve usability but may introduce additional risks. Long-term security involves making informed decisions regarding which conveniences are acceptable and which protections should remain in place despite minor inconveniences.

Developing incident response habits improves resilience significantly. Security incidents should not be viewed as personal failures but as opportunities to respond effectively and learn valuable lessons. Users should understand basic response procedures such as changing passwords, terminating active sessions, reviewing account activity, reporting fraudulent content, contacting platform support, and notifying affected contacts when necessary. Preparedness reduces panic and improves outcomes during stressful situations.

Critical thinking remains one of the most powerful cybersecurity skills. Technology changes rapidly, but human psychology remains relatively consistent. Attackers depend upon assumptions, distractions, trust, and emotional reactions. Individuals who develop habits of verification, skepticism, and thoughtful analysis are far less likely to become victims. Asking simple questions such as "Does this make sense?" or "Can I verify this independently?" often prevents successful attacks.

Self-discipline is a recurring theme throughout cybersecurity. Strong security practices frequently involve small actions performed consistently. Reviewing permissions, updating software, verifying messages, managing passwords, and evaluating content before posting may seem insignificant individually. However, these habits accumulate over time and create substantial protection. Security is often less about extraordinary actions and more about ordinary actions performed reliably.

The concept of digital citizenship extends beyond personal protection. Responsible social media users contribute to safer online communities by reporting scams, educating others, respecting privacy, and modeling secure behavior. Security awareness spreads through communities much like any other form of knowledge. Individuals who share accurate information and encourage responsible practices help strengthen the broader digital ecosystem.

Technology will continue evolving. New social media platforms, artificial intelligence tools, communication methods, and cybersecurity challenges will emerge. While specific threats may change, the principles of awareness, preparation, verification, privacy, and responsibility will remain relevant. Users who build strong habits today will be better prepared to navigate future technological environments safely.

Ultimately, long-term social media security is about maintaining control. Control over personal information. Control over digital identities. Control over online relationships. Control over how technology influences daily life. Building resilient habits empowers individuals to enjoy the benefits of social media while minimizing risks and adapting confidently to an ever-changing digital landscape.

The goal is not perfection. No security system can eliminate all risks. Instead, the objective is continuous improvement through awareness, education, and responsible behavior. Every positive habit strengthens resilience. Every informed decision reduces vulnerability. Over time, these habits create a foundation for safe, confident, and sustainable participation in the digital world.

Nathan had been using social media for nearly twenty years

He joined his first platform as a teenager and continued expanding his digital presence throughout adulthood. Over the years, he created accounts on numerous social networks, shared thousands of photographs, built professional connections, promoted business ventures, and maintained relationships with friends around the world.

Like many people, Nathan viewed social media as a normal part of life.

For a long time, cybersecurity was not something he thought about regularly. He used strong passwords on some accounts, weaker passwords on others, and occasionally ignored security recommendations because they seemed inconvenient.

Nothing serious happened.

At least, not at first.

Over time, however, Nathan experienced several minor incidents. A phishing email nearly fooled him. A fake profile impersonated one of his friends. A password appeared in a public data breach. A suspicious application requested excessive permissions on his smartphone.

Individually, none of these events caused major damage.

Collectively, they changed how he viewed digital security.

One evening, after reading about a large-scale social media breach affecting millions of users, Nathan decided to conduct a personal security review.

The results surprised him.

Several old accounts remained active even though he no longer used them. Some contained outdated personal information. Others were connected to obsolete email addresses. A few still used passwords created years earlier.

His digital life had become cluttered.

Determined to improve his security posture, Nathan created a simple plan.

Each month, he would review a portion of his digital ecosystem. One month focused on passwords. Another focused on privacy settings. Another involved reviewing connected applications and account permissions.

The process was manageable because he approached it gradually rather than attempting to fix everything at once.

As months passed, these activities became habits.

Nathan updated recovery information, enabled multi-factor authentication across all major accounts, and removed unnecessary applications. He reviewed old social media posts and deleted content that revealed excessive personal information.

More importantly, he developed a new mindset.

Instead of reacting to cybersecurity problems after they occurred, he began preventing them before they emerged.

One afternoon, his teenage daughter Emma approached him with a concern.

A stranger had contacted her through a social media platform claiming to be a modeling recruiter. The individual offered exciting opportunities and requested additional photographs.

Years earlier, Nathan might not have recognized the warning signs immediately.

Now, his cybersecurity awareness helped him identify the situation as a likely scam.

Together, they reported the account and discussed online safety principles.

That conversation became the beginning of regular family discussions about digital security.

Nathan taught his children how to recognize phishing messages, evaluate friend requests, protect personal information, and verify unusual claims. His wife became more involved in reviewing privacy settings and monitoring online activity as well.

The entire family became more resilient.

Several years later, Nathan's company experienced a social engineering attack targeting employees through social media platforms. Attackers created fake profiles impersonating executives and attempted to collect sensitive information from staff members.

Many employees were caught off guard.

Nathan was not.

His habit of verification immediately raised suspicions. Instead of responding, he contacted the executive through official channels and confirmed the messages were fraudulent.

Because he reported the activity quickly, the organization responded before significant damage occurred.

Experiences like these reinforced the value of long-term security habits.

Nathan realized that cybersecurity was not a destination. There was no point at which a person could declare themselves permanently secure and stop paying attention. The digital world changed too quickly for that.

Instead, security resembled physical fitness.

Regular exercise produces lasting benefits.

Ignoring health entirely creates vulnerabilities.

Consistency matters more than perfection.

The same principle applied to cybersecurity.

Years later, Nathan looked back on the changes he had made. None of them were particularly dramatic. He had not become a cybersecurity expert or invested in expensive technologies.

What changed were his habits.

He paused before clicking suspicious links.

He reviewed privacy settings regularly.

He maintained strong authentication practices.

He educated family members.

He verified information before trusting it.

He treated cybersecurity as a normal part of life rather than an occasional concern.

Those habits provided protection far beyond any individual security tool.

Most importantly, they provided confidence.

Nathan continued using social media for business, communication, education, and entertainment. He enjoyed technology without constantly fearing cyber threats because he understood how to manage risks responsibly.

The digital world remained imperfect. Scams still existed. New threats continued emerging. Cybercriminals remained active.

Yet Nathan knew something important.

Resilience is not the absence of challenges.

Resilience is the ability to face challenges successfully.

By building strong habits and maintaining awareness, he transformed from a passive technology user into an informed digital citizen capable of protecting himself and helping others do the same.

His journey demonstrated a powerful lesson that applies to everyone who uses social media: lasting security is not created by a single decision. It is built through thousands of small decisions made consistently over time.

Each secure password.

Each privacy review.

Each verified message.

Each thoughtful post.

Each security update.

Together, these actions create a resilient foundation capable of supporting safe and confident participation in the connected world.

And in a future where technology continues evolving faster than ever, that resilience may be one of the most valuable skills a person can possess.

Chapter 8

Responding to Social Media Security Incidents and Recovering From Account Compromises

No matter how careful a person may be, security incidents can still occur. Even users who maintain strong passwords, enable multi-factor authentication, avoid suspicious links, and follow cybersecurity best practices may eventually encounter account compromises, phishing attacks, identity theft attempts, device theft, or unauthorized access incidents. Cybersecurity is not about achieving perfect protection. Instead, it is about reducing risk, recognizing problems quickly, responding effectively, and recovering efficiently. Understanding how to respond to social media security incidents is a critical skill that can significantly limit damage and restore control over digital accounts and personal information.

One of the first principles of incident response is recognizing that speed matters. The sooner a security issue is identified, the greater the likelihood of limiting its impact. Many social media compromises continue for days or weeks because victims fail to notice unusual activity. Early detection often prevents attackers from gaining deeper access to accounts, contacting friends and followers, stealing sensitive information, or expanding their attacks to connected services.

Common warning signs of account compromise include login notifications from unfamiliar devices, password reset emails that were not requested, unusual posts appearing on profiles, messages sent without authorization, changes to account settings, missing content, unfamiliar friend requests, and complaints from contacts regarding suspicious activity. Users should take these indicators seriously and investigate immediately rather than assuming they are harmless errors.

When a compromise is suspected, the first priority is securing access to the account. If access remains available, users should immediately change their passwords and enable stronger authentication measures if they are not already active. Passwords should be unique, strong, and different from any previously used credentials. If the compromised password was reused on other services, those accounts should also be reviewed and updated. Attackers frequently test stolen credentials across multiple platforms in an effort to gain broader access.

Multi-factor authentication becomes particularly valuable during recovery efforts. If not previously enabled, users should activate it immediately after regaining control of an account. If multi-factor authentication was already active, users should verify that backup methods, recovery options, and trusted devices remain secure. Attackers sometimes modify recovery settings to maintain persistence even after passwords are changed.

Active session management is another critical recovery step. Most social media platforms allow users to review currently logged-in devices and terminate sessions remotely. This feature enables users to force all devices to reauthenticate, effectively removing unauthorized users from active sessions. Logging out all devices after a compromise helps ensure that attackers cannot continue accessing accounts using previously established connections.

Users should carefully review account settings following a security incident. Attackers often modify information such as email addresses, phone numbers, recovery methods, linked accounts, privacy settings, advertising permissions, and connected applications. These changes may allow attackers to regain access later or continue exploiting compromised accounts. Restoring account settings to trusted configurations is an important part of the recovery process.

Third-party application access deserves special attention after a compromise. Many social media platforms integrate with external services such as games, productivity tools, shopping applications, business software, and content management systems. Attackers may exploit these connections or create unauthorized integrations during a compromise. Reviewing and removing suspicious or unnecessary applications helps eliminate additional attack pathways.

Phishing-related compromises require additional investigation. If credentials were entered into a fraudulent website, users should determine exactly what information was exposed. Attackers may have obtained usernames, passwords, email addresses, authentication codes, payment information, or other sensitive data. Understanding the scope of exposure helps guide recovery decisions and informs additional protective actions.

Device security should also be evaluated during incident response. Compromised accounts may result from malware infections, malicious applications, browser vulnerabilities, or unauthorized device access. Running security scans, reviewing installed applications, updating software, and checking for suspicious activity can help identify underlying causes. Simply changing account credentials may not solve the problem if the device itself remains compromised.

Communication plays an important role in incident recovery. If attackers used a compromised account to contact friends, family members, followers, customers, or business associates, users should notify affected individuals as soon as possible. Warning contacts about fraudulent messages helps prevent secondary victims and limits reputational damage. Transparency often strengthens trust during recovery efforts.

Identity theft concerns should be evaluated whenever personal information may have been exposed. Depending on the nature of the compromise, attackers may gain access to names, addresses, phone numbers, financial information, photographs, personal documents, or private communications. Users should monitor financial accounts, review credit reports, watch for suspicious activity, and consider additional identity protection measures when appropriate.

Social media platforms typically provide recovery tools designed to assist users following account compromises. These tools may include identity verification processes, account restoration procedures, support channels, and security reviews. Familiarizing yourself with platform recovery resources before an incident occurs can simplify future recovery efforts. Knowing where to find assistance reduces stress during emergencies.

Emotional responses are natural during security incidents. Victims often experience anxiety, embarrassment, frustration, anger, or fear. These emotions can lead to impulsive decisions that complicate recovery efforts. Maintaining a calm, methodical approach improves outcomes significantly. Incident response should focus on facts, evidence, and systematic recovery rather than emotional reactions.

Documentation is a valuable but often overlooked component of incident management. Recording timelines, screenshots, suspicious messages, login notifications, unauthorized transactions, and support communications creates useful evidence. Documentation may assist with platform investigations, law enforcement reports, financial disputes, insurance claims, or future security reviews.

Learning from incidents is one of the most important aspects of digital resilience. Every security event provides opportunities to identify weaknesses, improve defenses, and strengthen future protection. Instead of viewing compromises solely as failures, users should treat them as educational experiences that reveal vulnerabilities requiring attention. Continuous improvement is a core principle of effective cybersecurity.

Organizations, influencers, and business owners may face additional responsibilities following social media incidents. Compromised business accounts can affect customers, employees, partners, and stakeholders. Recovery efforts may require public communication, customer notifications, advertising reviews, content restoration, and reputation management activities. Having predefined response plans can significantly improve organizational resilience.

The concept of layered security becomes especially relevant during incident response. No single security measure provides complete protection. Strong passwords, multi-factor authentication, secure devices, privacy controls, user education, software updates, and responsible behavior work together to reduce risk. When one layer fails, others often help contain damage and support recovery.

Long-term recovery extends beyond immediate account restoration. Users should continue monitoring affected accounts for unusual activity, review security settings regularly, update credentials when necessary, and remain alert for follow-up attacks. Cybercriminals frequently target previous victims because they assume successful compromises may indicate future opportunities. Ongoing vigilance helps prevent repeat incidents.

Ultimately, responding effectively to social media security incidents requires preparation, awareness, and resilience. Security challenges are an inevitable part of participating in digital environments. Users who understand recovery processes, maintain strong security practices, and approach incidents methodically are far better equipped to overcome setbacks and restore control quickly. Recovery is not simply about regaining access to an account—it is about rebuilding trust, improving security, and emerging stronger than before.

Lauren immediately realized something was wrong

Lauren had spent nearly a decade building her online presence.

As a travel blogger and content creator, social media served as both a personal passion and a professional business. Her accounts contained years of photographs, partnerships, customer communications, and valuable relationships with followers around the world.

One morning, everything changed.

When Lauren opened her primary social media application, she was unable to log in.

At first, she assumed she had mistyped her password. After several unsuccessful attempts, she requested a password reset. The recovery email never arrived.

Concerned, she checked her inbox more carefully.

There she found a notification indicating that her account email address had been changed several hours earlier.

Lauren immediately realized something was wrong.

Panic set in as she searched for her profile from another device. The account was still active, but recent posts promoted cryptocurrency investments and suspicious financial opportunities. Friends had already begun asking questions.

Someone had taken control of her account.

For several minutes, Lauren felt overwhelmed. Years of work appeared to be disappearing before her eyes. Fortunately, she remembered a cybersecurity webinar she had attended months earlier. One of the presenters emphasized the importance of staying calm during security incidents.

Taking a deep breath, Lauren began following a structured recovery process.

First, she documented everything. Screenshots captured unauthorized posts, account changes, and notification emails.

She recorded timestamps and preserved evidence that might later prove useful.

Next, she initiated the platform's account recovery procedure.

The process required identity verification, submission of supporting information, and several security checks. Although frustrating, the system was designed to help legitimate users regain access after compromises.

While waiting for support responses, Lauren reviewed other online accounts.

The investigation quickly revealed that attackers had accessed her email account first. From there, they used password reset features to compromise her social media profile. The social media account itself had not been the original target.

Fortunately, Lauren regained access to her email before additional damage occurred.

She immediately changed passwords, enabled multi-factor authentication, reviewed recovery options, and terminated all active sessions. These actions prevented attackers from maintaining access to connected services.

Several days later, the social media platform restored her account.

The recovery process was not complete, however.

Attackers had modified privacy settings, connected unauthorized applications, and altered business information. Lauren spent hours reviewing every setting carefully and restoring proper configurations.

She also posted a public explanation for followers.

Rather than hiding the incident, Lauren explained what happened and warned others about similar attacks. The response was overwhelmingly supportive. Many followers shared stories of their own experiences with phishing attempts, fake profiles, and compromised accounts.

The incident became an opportunity for education.

Months later, Lauren received another suspicious email claiming that her account had violated platform policies and would be suspended immediately unless she verified her credentials.

The message appeared convincing.

Before the compromise, she might have clicked without hesitation.

Now, she recognized several warning signs immediately.

The sender's address was unusual. The language created artificial urgency. The login link pointed to an unfamiliar domain.

It was another phishing attack.

Lauren deleted the message and reported it.

The experience reinforced an important lesson: recovery does not end when an account is restored. Security awareness must continue afterward.

Over the next year, Lauren strengthened every aspect of her digital security. She implemented password management software, enabled authentication across all major accounts, reviewed privacy settings regularly, and maintained secure backups of important content.

She also created an incident response checklist.

The document outlined exactly what actions to take if future security problems occurred. Contact information, recovery procedures, account inventories, backup locations, and response steps were organized in advance.

Having a plan provided peace of mind.

One evening, a fellow content creator named Alex contacted Lauren in distress. His account had been compromised, and he did not know where to begin.

Lauren shared her recovery checklist and walked him through the process step by step.

Document the incident.

Secure email access.

Change passwords.

Review active sessions.

Enable multi-factor authentication.

Notify followers.

Contact platform support.

Review connected applications.

Monitor ongoing activity.

Within days, Alex regained control of his account.

The experience reminded Lauren how valuable preparation could be during stressful situations.

Years later, Lauren viewed the account compromise differently than she had on the day it occurred. At the time, it felt catastrophic. In retrospect, it became one of the most important learning experiences of her digital life.

The incident exposed weaknesses she did not know existed.

It forced her to develop stronger habits.

It improved her understanding of cybersecurity.

It allowed her to help others facing similar challenges.

Most importantly, it taught her that resilience matters more than perfection.

No one can eliminate all risks from the digital world.

Accounts may be targeted.

Devices may be lost.

Scams may appear convincing.

New threats will continue emerging.

The goal is not to guarantee that problems never occur.

The goal is to recognize problems quickly, respond effectively, recover efficiently, and emerge stronger than before.

Lauren continued building her online business successfully. She remained active on social media, collaborated with brands, and connected with audiences around the world. The difference was that she now approached digital security as an ongoing responsibility rather than an afterthought.

Her experience demonstrated a powerful truth about cybersecurity: incidents do not define users. Responses do.

With preparation, awareness, and resilience, even significant setbacks can become opportunities for growth, learning, and stronger protection in the future.

And in the ever-changing world of social media, that resilience may be the most valuable security tool of all.

Chapter 9

The Future of Social Media Security, Artificial Intelligence, and Digital Identity Protection

Social media has evolved dramatically since its early beginnings. What started as simple online communities for sharing messages and photographs has transformed into a global ecosystem connecting billions of people, businesses, governments, organizations, and technologies. Mobile devices now serve as the primary gateway to these platforms, making social media an integral part of modern life. As technology continues advancing, social media security must evolve alongside it. Understanding future trends, emerging threats, and new security technologies is essential for protecting digital identities in an increasingly connected world.

One of the most significant developments shaping the future of social media security is artificial intelligence. AI systems are becoming more capable every year. These technologies can analyze vast amounts of data, identify behavioral patterns, automate decision-making, and generate highly realistic digital content. Artificial intelligence offers tremendous opportunities for improving cybersecurity, but it also creates powerful tools that can be exploited by cybercriminals. The future of social media security will involve an ongoing competition between defensive AI systems and malicious AI-powered attacks.

AI-driven security tools already help social media platforms detect suspicious behavior. Machine learning algorithms can analyze login patterns, identify unusual activity, detect automated bot networks, recognize phishing campaigns, and flag potentially fraudulent accounts. These systems operate continuously and can process information at scales impossible for human analysts alone. As AI technology improves, automated threat detection will become even more effective at identifying malicious behavior before significant damage occurs.

At the same time, cybercriminals are adopting artificial intelligence for offensive purposes. AI-generated phishing messages are becoming increasingly sophisticated. Traditional phishing attacks often contained grammatical errors, awkward language, or obvious warning signs. Modern AI systems can produce highly convincing messages tailored to specific individuals, organizations, or situations. These personalized attacks may be difficult to distinguish from legitimate communications, increasing the importance of verification and critical thinking.

Deepfake technology represents another emerging challenge. Deepfakes use artificial intelligence to create realistic images, videos, and audio recordings that depict events that never actually occurred. Attackers can use deepfakes to impersonate public figures, business executives, family members, or trusted contacts. A convincing video or voice recording may be used to spread misinformation, manipulate public opinion, commit fraud, or conduct social engineering attacks. As deepfake technology improves, users must learn to evaluate digital content more critically and verify information through trusted sources.

Digital identity protection is becoming increasingly important as social media profiles evolve into comprehensive representations of individuals. A digital identity includes personal information, social connections, online activities, professional histories, financial interactions, preferences, photographs, communications, and behavioral patterns. This digital identity often influences employment opportunities, business relationships, educational prospects, and personal reputations. Protecting digital identity will become one of the central cybersecurity challenges of the coming decades.

Identity theft is likely to become more sophisticated in the future. Rather than simply stealing account credentials, attackers may attempt to replicate entire digital identities.

AI-generated profiles, deepfake media, and automated impersonation tools could allow criminals to create convincing digital duplicates of real individuals. These impersonations may be used to deceive friends, customers, employers, or financial institutions. Strong authentication systems and identity verification technologies will play critical roles in defending against these threats.

Biometric authentication is expected to become increasingly common across social media platforms and mobile devices. Fingerprints, facial recognition, voice authentication, behavioral analysis, and other biometric technologies offer alternatives to traditional passwords. While biometrics can improve convenience and security, they also introduce new privacy concerns. Unlike passwords, biometric characteristics cannot easily be changed if compromised. Future systems will need to balance security benefits with privacy protections carefully.

Decentralized identity systems are emerging as potential solutions to some modern privacy challenges. Traditional digital identities are often controlled by large platforms and centralized databases. Decentralized systems seek to give users greater control over personal information by allowing individuals to manage their own identity credentials. While these technologies remain in development, they may eventually provide users with stronger privacy protections and greater ownership of personal data.

Privacy regulations are likely to continue evolving worldwide. Governments and regulatory organizations increasingly recognize the importance of protecting personal information. Future regulations may impose stricter requirements regarding data collection, storage, sharing, transparency, and user consent. Social media users should remain informed about privacy rights and understand how evolving regulations affect their digital experiences.

The Internet of Things, often referred to as IoT, will further expand social media security considerations. Smart devices such as watches, fitness trackers, vehicles, home assistants, cameras, and appliances generate enormous amounts of data. Many of these devices connect directly or indirectly to social media platforms. As interconnected technologies become more common, securing digital identities will require protecting a broader ecosystem of devices and services.

Augmented reality and virtual reality technologies are also influencing the future of social media. These immersive environments may create new opportunities for communication, education, business, and entertainment. However, they will also introduce new security challenges involving identity verification, virtual asset protection, privacy management, behavioral tracking, and social engineering attacks. Users must prepare for security risks that extend beyond traditional text, photographs, and videos.

Data ownership will remain a major topic of discussion. Social media platforms collect extensive information regarding user behavior, preferences, interactions, locations, and activities. Questions surrounding who owns this data, how it may be used, and how long it should be retained will continue shaping technology policies and user expectations. Understanding data ownership principles helps users make informed decisions regarding participation in digital ecosystems.

Cybersecurity education will become increasingly important as technologies grow more complex. Technical solutions alone cannot eliminate risks. Users must understand how digital systems function, recognize emerging threats, evaluate information critically, and make responsible decisions. Lifelong learning will become an essential component of digital citizenship. Those who remain informed and adaptable will be better prepared to navigate future technological environments safely.

Social media companies are expected to invest heavily in trust and safety technologies. Content moderation systems, fraud detection tools, account protection mechanisms, and identity verification processes will continue improving. However, no platform can guarantee complete protection. Users must remain active participants in their own security rather than relying entirely on platform providers.

The concept of digital reputation will likely become even more significant in the future. Employers, educational institutions, customers, investors, and professional networks increasingly evaluate individuals based on online presence and digital behavior. Managing digital reputations responsibly requires understanding how information persists online and how digital identities evolve over time. Thoughtful participation in social media communities contributes to long-term personal and professional success.

Resilience remains one of the most valuable qualities in cybersecurity. Technology will continue changing. New threats will emerge. Attack techniques will evolve. Security tools will improve. Users who cultivate adaptability, awareness, critical thinking, and responsible habits will be better positioned to respond successfully to future challenges. Resilience allows individuals to navigate uncertainty without becoming overwhelmed by change.

Ethics will play an increasingly important role in digital security. Artificial intelligence, identity technologies, content moderation systems, and privacy tools raise important questions regarding fairness, accountability, transparency, and human rights. Responsible use of technology benefits individuals and society as a whole. Understanding ethical considerations helps users make informed decisions while contributing positively to digital communities.

Ultimately, the future of social media security is not solely about technology. It is about people. Human behavior, decision-making, relationships, trust, education, and responsibility remain central factors in cybersecurity. Technology may change dramatically, but the need for awareness, preparation, and thoughtful participation will remain constant.

The future will undoubtedly bring new opportunities and challenges. By understanding emerging technologies, protecting digital identities, maintaining strong security habits, and embracing lifelong learning, users can confidently participate in the next generation of social media and digital communication. The goal is not to fear the future but to prepare for it intelligently and responsibly.

Ethan always loved technology

As a teenager, he spent countless hours exploring social media platforms, creating content, and experimenting with new applications. By the time he reached adulthood, digital communication had become deeply integrated into nearly every aspect of his personal and professional life.

Technology fascinated him.

The rapid pace of innovation seemed limitless.

Every year introduced new devices, platforms, applications, and possibilities.

Yet as exciting as these developments were, Ethan also noticed a growing number of cybersecurity concerns. News reports frequently described data breaches, identity theft incidents, phishing campaigns, and increasingly sophisticated scams.

One evening, while browsing social media, Ethan encountered a video featuring a well-known entrepreneur promoting an investment opportunity.

The video appeared completely authentic.

The entrepreneur's appearance, voice, expressions, and mannerisms were perfectly recognizable.

Thousands of people had already shared the content.

Something about the presentation seemed unusual, however.

Instead of investing immediately, Ethan researched further.

Within hours, cybersecurity experts revealed that the video was entirely fabricated using deepfake technology.

The entrepreneur had never recorded the message.

The investment opportunity was a scam.

The experience left a strong impression on Ethan.

If technology could create such convincing deception, how would people distinguish reality from manipulation in the future?

Motivated by curiosity, Ethan enrolled in several cybersecurity and artificial intelligence courses. He wanted to understand both the opportunities and risks associated with emerging technologies.

As he studied, he discovered that artificial intelligence was transforming nearly every aspect of cybersecurity.

AI systems helped identify threats, analyze network activity, detect fraud, and protect users.

At the same time, attackers used AI to automate scams, generate fake content, and conduct highly personalized social engineering attacks.

The future would involve both sides leveraging increasingly powerful technologies.

Several years later, Ethan launched a digital consulting business specializing in online security awareness. His clients included small businesses, entrepreneurs, educators, and content creators.

One client, Maria, approached him with a troubling problem.

Someone had created an AI-generated clone of her online identity.

The attackers copied photographs, videos, writing samples, and public information from her social media profiles. Using artificial intelligence, they created realistic content that appeared to come directly from her.

Followers became confused.

Some customers questioned which account was authentic.

The situation demonstrated how digital identity theft had evolved beyond traditional account compromises.

Together, Ethan and Maria implemented identity verification measures, strengthened account security, and educated followers about the risks of digital impersonation.

The experience reinforced an important lesson.

Protecting digital identity would become increasingly important as technology advanced.

Over the next decade, Ethan watched social media evolve dramatically.

Biometric authentication became commonplace.

AI-driven security systems improved threat detection.

Privacy regulations expanded.

Virtual reality social platforms gained popularity.

Smart devices integrated seamlessly with online identities.

The digital world grew more sophisticated and interconnected.

Despite these changes, Ethan noticed something remarkable.

The most effective security principles remained largely unchanged.

Verify information.

Protect personal data.

Think critically.

Use strong authentication.

Maintain awareness.

Continue learning.

Technology changed.

Human psychology remained surprisingly consistent.

One afternoon, Ethan spoke at a cybersecurity conference attended by students preparing for careers in technology.

A participant asked an interesting question.

"What do you think will be the biggest cybersecurity challenge in the future?"

Ethan paused before answering.

Many people expected him to mention artificial intelligence, quantum computing, or some other advanced technology.

Instead, he offered a different perspective.

"The biggest challenge," he said, "will be helping people understand and adapt to change."

The audience listened carefully.

"Technology evolves rapidly. Security tools evolve. Threats evolve. But people often resist learning new habits. The individuals who succeed in the future won't necessarily be the most technical. They'll be the most adaptable."

Years later, Ethan reflected on that conversation.

He realized that resilience had become the defining characteristic of successful digital citizens.

The most secure people were not those who never encountered threats.

They were the people who recognized risks, learned continuously, adapted effectively, and recovered when problems occurred.

As artificial intelligence became more powerful and digital identities more valuable, these qualities grew increasingly important.

Ethan remained optimistic about the future.

Yes, new threats would emerge.

Deepfakes would improve.

Identity theft would evolve.

Social engineering attacks would become more sophisticated.

But defensive technologies would improve as well.

Education would expand.

Awareness would increase.

Users would develop stronger security habits.

The future was not predetermined.

It would be shaped by the choices individuals made every day.

By protecting identities, respecting privacy, embracing learning, and using technology responsibly, people could enjoy the benefits of innovation while minimizing risks.

Standing in his office one evening, Ethan looked at the countless technological advances that had transformed society during his lifetime.

The future promised even greater change.

Yet one lesson remained constant.

Technology is a tool.

How people use it ultimately determines whether it becomes a source of opportunity or vulnerability.

The responsibility belongs to all of us.

And that responsibility begins with awareness, continues through education, and grows through every decision we make in the digital world.

As social media, artificial intelligence, and digital identities continue evolving together, those who remain informed, adaptable, and resilient will be best prepared to thrive in whatever future awaits.

how people use it ultimately determines whether it becomes a source of opportunity or vulnerability.

The responsibility belongs to all of us.

And that responsibility begins with awareness, continues through education, and grows through every decision we make in the digital world.

As social media, artificial intelligence, and digital identities continue evolving together, those who remain informed, adaptable, and resilient will be best prepared to thrive in whatever future awaits.

Final Thoughts: Building a Lifetime of Social Media Security and Digital Confidence

The world has changed dramatically in a relatively short period of time. Just a few decades ago, social interactions occurred primarily through face-to-face conversations, telephone calls, letters, and local communities. Today, billions of people communicate, share experiences, conduct business, learn, entertain themselves, and build relationships through social media platforms accessible from the smartphones they carry every day. Social media has become one of the most powerful communication tools ever created, connecting individuals across countries, cultures, languages, and industries in ways that previous generations could scarcely imagine.

With these incredible opportunities comes responsibility. Throughout this book, we have explored the many ways social media can expose users to risks involving privacy violations, phishing attacks, scams, fake profiles, account takeovers, identity theft, malware infections, misinformation, and emerging threats powered by artificial intelligence. These risks are real and continue evolving every year. However, the purpose of understanding these threats is not to create fear. The goal is to create awareness, confidence, and preparedness.

Cybersecurity is often misunderstood as a highly technical field reserved for programmers, hackers, engineers, and IT professionals. In reality, many of the most effective security practices require no advanced technical expertise at all. They involve habits, awareness, decision-making, and personal responsibility. Strong passwords, multi-factor authentication, careful content sharing, privacy management, scam awareness, software updates, and thoughtful online behavior provide powerful protection that is available to virtually every user. Technology plays an important role, but human behavior remains one of the most important factors in cybersecurity success.

One of the most valuable lessons in social media security is recognizing the value of personal information. Every social media profile represents far more than a collection of photographs and posts. It contains pieces of identity, relationships, interests, experiences, routines, preferences, and memories. Information that appears insignificant in isolation may become highly valuable when combined with other publicly available data. Understanding this reality helps users make more informed decisions about what they share, who can view it, and how it may be used in the future.

Privacy should not be viewed as secrecy. Privacy is about maintaining control. It means deciding how personal information is collected, shared, stored, and accessed. Every user deserves the ability to control their digital identity and determine what aspects of their lives remain public or private. Social media platforms offer powerful opportunities for connection, but those opportunities should never require sacrificing personal security or dignity.

As technology continues evolving, new challenges will undoubtedly emerge. Artificial intelligence is already transforming how people create content, communicate, and interact online. While AI offers remarkable benefits, it also introduces new forms of deception, impersonation, misinformation, and fraud. Deepfake technology, automated phishing campaigns, synthetic identities, and AI-generated scams will continue becoming more sophisticated. Yet the fundamental defenses remain the same: verification, critical thinking, awareness, and responsible decision-making.

One of the most important concepts discussed throughout this book is resilience. Resilience is the ability to adapt, recover, and continue moving forward despite challenges. No security system can eliminate every risk. No technology can guarantee complete protection. Even the most careful users may eventually encounter suspicious messages, phishing attempts, privacy concerns, or security incidents. What matters most is how individuals respond. Prepared users recognize problems quickly, take appropriate action, learn from experiences, and strengthen their defenses moving forward.

Social media security is not a destination that users reach once and then forget. It is an ongoing journey. New platforms appear. Existing platforms introduce new features. Privacy settings change. Threats evolve. Security tools improve. The digital landscape remains dynamic. Lifelong learning and continuous awareness are essential for maintaining strong protection over time. Users who remain curious, informed, and adaptable are far better positioned to navigate future challenges successfully.

Families have a particularly important role in promoting digital safety. Children and teenagers are growing up in a world where social media is often present from an early age. Teaching younger generations about privacy, security, online behavior, and digital responsibility helps create safer online communities for everyone. These lessons are not merely technical skills; they are life skills that will remain valuable throughout adulthood. Parents, educators, mentors, and community leaders all contribute to building stronger digital citizens.

Businesses and professionals must also recognize the importance of social media security. Online identities often serve as extensions of personal and professional reputations. A compromised account can affect customers, colleagues, business partners, and communities. Whether operating a small business, managing a professional network, building a personal brand, or simply communicating with friends, every user benefits from adopting a security-focused mindset.

Throughout history, every major technological advancement has introduced both opportunities and risks. The internet is no different. Social media can strengthen relationships, expand knowledge, support businesses, promote creativity, and create meaningful connections across the globe. These benefits are significant and worth preserving. The goal of cybersecurity is not to discourage participation but to enable safe participation.

Responsible digital citizenship extends beyond personal protection. Every informed user contributes to the security of the broader online ecosystem. Reporting scams, educating others, respecting privacy, verifying information, and modeling responsible behavior all help create safer digital environments. Security is not solely an individual responsibility; it is also a community effort. Small actions performed by millions of users collectively strengthen online safety for everyone.

As you complete this book, remember that cybersecurity is ultimately about empowerment. Knowledge provides confidence. Awareness reduces vulnerability. Preparation improves resilience. Strong habits create lasting protection. Every step you take toward improving your security strengthens your ability to enjoy the benefits of social media without unnecessary risk.

The smartphone in your pocket connects you to a vast digital world filled with opportunities, relationships, information, and experiences. By applying the principles discussed throughout this book, you can navigate that world more safely and confidently. Protect your accounts. Guard your privacy. Think critically. Verify information. Continue learning. Most importantly, remember that technology should serve you—not control you.

The future of social media will continue evolving in exciting and unpredictable ways. New innovations will emerge. New opportunities will appear. New challenges will arise. Yet users who build strong foundations based on awareness, responsibility, and resilience will always be better prepared to thrive in whatever digital future awaits.

Your social media accounts represent more than technology. They represent your voice, your relationships, your experiences, your reputation, and your identity. Protect them wisely. Use them responsibly. And approach every online interaction with the confidence that comes from being informed, prepared, and empowered.

Thank you for joining this journey through Social Media Security for Mobile Devices. May the knowledge you have gained help you build a safer, smarter, and more secure digital future for yourself and those around you.

Your social media accounts represent more than technology. They represent your voice, your relationships, your experiences, your reputation, and your identity. Protect them wisely. Use them responsibly. And approach every online interaction with the confidence that comes from being informed, prepared, and empowered.

Thank you for joining this journey through Social Media Security for Mobile Devices. May the knowledge you have gained help you build a safer, smarter, and more secure digital future for yourself and those around you.

www.ingramcontent.com/pod-product-compliance
Lightning Source LLC
LaVergne TN
LVHW030726061126
851857LV00019B/2016